CISTERCIAN FATHERS SERIES: NUMBER SIXTY-ONE

Helinand of Froidmont

Verses on Death

CISTERCIAN FATHERS SERIES: NUMBER SIXTY-ONE

The Verses on Death
of
Helinand of Froidmont

Les Vers de la Mort

Old French Text with
Verse Translation and Commentary
by
Jenny Lind Porter

Introduction by William D. Paden

Cistercian Publications
Kalamazoo, Michigan – Spencer, Massachusetts
1999

The editors express their appreciation to the Fellows of the
Société des Anciens Texte Français
for their permission to reproduce the Old French text,
edited by Fr. Wulff et Em. Walberg
and published as
Les Vers de la Mort par Hélinant, Moine de Froidmont
Paris: Librairie de Firmin Didot et Cie, 1905

Cistercian Publications (Editorial Offices)
The Institute of Cistercian Studies
Western Michigan University
Kalamazoo 49008

Available from Cistercian Publications (Distribution)
Saint Joseph's Abbey
Spencer, Massachusetts 01562
and
Cistercian Publications (UK)
Mount Saint Bernard Abbey
Coalville, Leicester LE67 5UL

*The work of Cistercian Publications is made possible in part
by support from Western Michigan University to
The Institute of Cistercian Studies*

Cataloguing in Publication data available upon request.

*Typeset by Bookcomp, Inc., Grand Rapids Michigan
Printed in the United States of America*

TABLE OF CONTENTS

Helinand's *Verses on Death* in Medieval Literature and Spirituality

William D. Paden

'It goes very ill with my second boy,
or rather well—since he is leaving the follies,
snares and dreams of this world, before he has been
caught by them.'
—Ser Lapo Mazzei, 1394

'Be consoled if [abbot Goswin] lives, since a dear father
is saved for you;
be consoled if he dies, since a powerful defender
is prepared for you.'
—Hugh, abbot of Saint-Amand, 1166

DEATH PROVOKED ambivalent responses from medieval people. On one hand, as creatures living in this world they feared death, as did Ser Lapo Mazzei when he wrote in a letter to a friend that his second son, stricken by plague, was doing badly. On the other hand, though, as Christians they saw Death as the portal into a better existence; so Ser Lapo, striving to console himself, could say in the same sentence that his boy was doing well, since he was dying to this world.[1] The same poles of ambivalence may be detected in monastic thought, as when Hugh of Saint-Amand attempted to console the

[1] 'Un mio fanciullo mezzano . . . sta molto male, anzi molto bene, ch'esce di queste pazzie e viluppi e sogni del mondo, anzi che s'avviluppi con esse': Cesare Guasti, ed., *Lettere di un notaro ad un mercante del secolo XIV* (Florence: Le Monnier, 1880) vol. 1: p. 68. Trans. Iris Origo, *The Merchant of Prato: Daily Life in a Medieval Italian City* (London: Penguin, 1963) p. 216. For a portrait of 'the wise, kindly family friend, Ser Lapo Mazzei—the personification of the Tuscan virtues of piety and moderation,' see Origo, pp. 205–24 (this citation, p. 13).

monks of Anchin whether their abbot lived or died. Hugh implied that if the abbot lived, life was good and death was bad, but if he died then life was bad and death was good.[2]

This ambivalence pervades medieval literature of death, including the *Verses on Death* by Helinand, the Cistercian monk of Froidmont. Helinand composed the poem in the mid-1190s, between 1193 or 1194 and 1197.[3] We know that he had become a monk of Froidmont by 1190, and that he probably entered the monastery around 1182.[4] Elsewhere he tells us that he had enjoyed success as a poet before becoming a monk, so the two obvious contexts for the *Verses*, his only extant work in French, are french poetry of the twelfth century and the monastic tradition. But the *Verses* do not fit either context easily. On the one hand, they differ from worldly french poetry of the time by their unmistakable monastic imprint. At the end of the poem Helinand recoils from worldly debauchery and lust, saying that he prefers the monastic diet: 'I prefer my peas and my soup.'[5] The *Verses* treat Death in a way unparalleled in poetry of

[2]'Consolamini, consolamini, inquiens, populus meus; consolamini, si vixerit, quia Pater vobis charissimus conservatur: consolamini, si decesserit, quia Patronus vobis fortissimus praeparatur': *Acta Sanctorum*, October, vol. 4:1092 (rprt. Bruxelles: Culture et Civilisation, 1970). Quoted by H. Platelle, 'La mort précieuse: La mort des moines d'après quelques sources des Pays Bas du sud,' *Revue Mabillon* 60 (1981–84) 151–74, at p.161.

[3]The standard text of the poem was edited by Fr. Wulff and Em. Walberg, *Les vers de la mort par Hélinant, moine de Froidmont* (Paris: Firmin Didot, 1905). Wulff and Walberg (p. xv) date the text 1194–97, assuming that the 'two kings' of stanza XX were Philip Augustus and Richard Lionheart. I have argued elsewhere that they were instead Philip and Canute VI of Denmark (brother of Ingeburga, the wife whom Philip rejected), in which case the poem could have been written in 1193; see my study, '*De Monachis rithmos facientibus*: Hélinant de Froidmont, Bertran de Born, and the Cistercian General Chapter of 1199', *Speculum* 55 (1980) 669–85, at pp. 674–77.

[4]For charters he witnessed as a monk in 1190–98 see William D. Paden, 'Documents concernant Hélinant de Froidmont,' *Romania* 105 (1984) 332–41. For a recent review of Helinand's life see Beverly M. Kienzle, 'Hélinand de Froidmont et la prédication cistercienne dans le Midi (1145–1229),' *La prédication en Pays d'Oc (XIIe-début XVe siècle)*, Cahiers de Fanjeaux 32 (Toulouse: Privat, 1997) 37–67, at pp. 38–41.

[5]'Aim mieus mes pois et ma poree' (stanza 50, line 12). I quote Helinand in English from my translation in literal prose, 'The *Verses on Death* by Hélinant de Froidmont,' *Allegorica* 3.2 (1978) 62–103. For french translations in both verse and prose see Michel Boyer and Monique Santucci, trans., *Hélinand de Froidmont: Les Vers de la mort, poème du XIIe siècle* (Paris: Champion, 1983).

their own time, and anticipate the Dance of Death in the fifteenth century. On the other hand, the dark and threatening presence of death differs radically from the joyful experience of the soul entering upon eternal bliss as described by Saint Bernard.[6] If Helinand stands outside these two traditions, if his *Verses* are truly unparalleled, they defy our understanding. I suggest, however, that the poem is not radically *sui generis*, rather that it is an unusual combination of elements known elsewhere. I propose to consider various forms of medieval death-literature in order to triangulate the *Verses on Death* by comparing them with each one.

I
Medieval French Poetry of Death

What do we know about Helinand's career as a French poet? He tells us about it himself, briefly and allusively, in his *Chronicon*:

> Ipse quidem spectaculum factus est, et angelis et hominibus levitate miraculi, qui prius eis spectaculum fuerat levitatis; dum non scena, non circus, non theatrum, non amphitheatrum, non amphicircus, non forum, non platea, non gymnasium, non arena sine eo resonabat.[7]
>
> Indeed he made himself a spectacle to both angels and men by the levity of a miracle [i.e., his conversion], he who had been a spectacle of levity to them before, when no stage, no circus, no theatre, no amphitheatre, no amphicircus, no forum, no courtyard, no public school, no arena resounded without him.

Using classical vocabulary Helinand describes himself implicitly as an actor on the *scena* or *theatrum*, a gladiator in the *circus*, an orator in the *forum*, or a student in the *gymnasium*. Perhaps in his worldly days he was a performer, like an actor or a gladiator, or perhaps he

[6] See Jean Leclercq, 'La joie de mourir selon saint Bernard de Clairvaux,' *Dies Illa: Death in the Middle Ages*, ed. Jane H. M. Taylor (Liverpool: Francis Cairns, 1984), pp. 195–207. An english translation was published as 'The Joy of Dying According to Saint Bernard', *Cistercian Studies* [*Quarterly*] 25 (1990) 163–174.

[7] *Patrologia Latina* 212:748CD, cited by Kienzle, p. 61, n. 29.

was a performer and composer at once, like an orator or a student. It is natural, then, to suppose that in twelfth-century terms he may have been a *jongleur* (a performer of lyric or epic poetry) or a *trouvère* (a lyric poet), perhaps a *trouvère* who performed, especially in dialogue forms such as the *tenson* or the *jeu parti*. Perhaps he implies that he once sang of love, when, in the *Verses*, he directs Death to 'go to those who sing of love and boast of vain things, and teach them to sing' like monks.[8] We have, however, no french lyrics attributed to Helinand; he does not figure among two hundred sixty-odd trouvères whose names we know.[9] If he did write lyric verse he would have been among the earliest trouvères to do so. Helinand was born, perhaps, around 1162, and he died in 1237.[10] The earliest trouvères we know of were active about 1170,[11] so Helinand may have figured in the first generation at a time when french lyric poetry had only begun to gain sufficient recognition to be transcribed and transmitted. In any case, since none of the medieval french lyric genres focused on death, we have no french lyric verse that may serve as historical background for his vernacular work.

Since we only speculate that Helinand wrote lyric poetry at all, we must consider other genres in practice which could shed light on his treatment of death.[12] Among the monuments of early Old French

[8]Stanza 2, lines 1–6.

[9]See Robert White Linker, *A Bibliography of Old French Lyrics* (University, Mississippi: Romance Monographs, 1979).

[10]Kienzle, pp. 40–41.

[11]Guy Muraille, 'Trouvères lyriques,' in *Dictionnaire des lettres françaises: Le moyen âge*, 2nd ed., ed. Geneviève Hasenohr and Michel Zink (Paris: Fayard, 1992) p. 1459.

[12]On death in the *chansons de geste* see Paul Zumthor, 'Les *planctus* épiques,' *Romania* 84 (1963) 61–69. On death in french romances, Elisabeth Schulze-Busacker, 'Étude typologique de la complainte des morts dans le roman arthurien en vers du 12e au 14e siècle', *An Arthurian Tapestry: Essays in Memory of Lewis Thorpe*, ed. Kenneth Varty (Glasgow: French Department of the University of Glasgow, 1981) 54–68. The didactic *complainte* expressed lamentation for the death of a great figure such as King Louis VIII (1226, the earliest *complainte* preserved); it was practiced as late as the Grands Rhétoriqueurs in the fifteenth century. Several *complaintes* show influence of Helinand's *Verses on Death*; see Claude Thiry, *La plainte funèbre* (Turnhout: Brepols, 1978) 77–78. On the expression of grief in general see J. Frappier, 'La douleur et la mort dans la littérature française des XIIe et XIIIe siècles,' *Il dolore e la morte nella spiritualità medievale* (Todi: Accademia Tudertina, 1967) 67–110.

poetry two stand out in this regard, the *Song of Roland*, an epic narrative of a hero's death in battle, written down in the earliest version we have about 1100, and the *Life of Saint Alexis*, from about the same time.[13] These two texts, in the early versions, resemble each other in language (the Anglo-Norman dialect) and versification (the assonating decasyllable), but contrast in ethos. Both may be considered heroic, but the heroes are of two distinct kinds, one secular and the other sacred.

Accordingly the views of death implicit in the two texts make a clear contrast. Roland is betrayed by a traitor; his rear-guard is attacked by overwhelming numbers and reduced from twenty thousand men (with epic exaggeration) to sixty, then three, then two, then one. As a christian warrior he confesses his sins and, because he is the greatest christian warrior in the poem, his death is marked by the descent of a company of angels, led by Saint Michael, to receive his soul. Despite such angelic confirmation of his triumph, however, Roland's death is an occasion for grief, not joy. When Charlemagne returns to the field of battle at the head of his army, twenty thousand men weep for the death of the hero. Their grief and Charlemagne's justify their swift vengeance. For all its militant christian values, the song is profoundly secular.[14]

The *Life* of Saint Alexis narrates his conversion, suffering, and death. The son of a roman nobleman, Alexis realizes on his wedding night that the joys of this world are not for him. After attempting to explain this newfound insight to his baffled bride, he leaves Rome secretly and takes up the life of a holy wanderer. Eventually he returns, unrecognizable, and takes lodging as an unknown beggar in his parents' home beneath the servants' stairs, where he is regularly soaked in dirty water from the laundry. He declines in health and eventually dies, leaving a letter explaining who he is and why he has lived so long without revealing himself to his parents. When they learn this startling news, his parents go into paroxysms of grief.

[13]See Gerard J. Brault, ed., *The Song of Roland: An Analytical Edition*, 2 vols. (University Park: Pennsylvania State University Press, 1978); C. Storey, ed., *La vie de saint Alexis* (Oxford: Blackwell, 1968).

[14]For a fuller statement of this reading see William D. Paden, 'Tenebrism in the *Song of Roland*,' *Modern Philology* 86 (1989) 339–56.

His mother, in anguish, destroys the fine decorations in her bedroom, while his father grieves more inwardly. The people of Rome, however, rejoice in the discovery of a saint who will intercede for them. The poem leaves no doubt that the parents are wrong to grieve because they are short-sighted, limited in their perception to worldly concerns and unable to see the true meaning of the death of the saint.

The two texts show two contrasting views of death, the secular view in which death is bad and the sacred view which sees it as good. The contrast is mitigated on both sides: for the Roland-poet; his hero was such a powerful christian figure as to win a great show of divine approval. For the poet of Alexis, the parents' grief provided a moving spectacle. But we are left in no doubt as to which view each text ultimately endorses: the Roland secular and the Alexis sacred.

As the Middle Ages advanced, french literature showed concern with death in many ways. The stanza-form invented by Helinand was employed by several thirteenth-century poets who sang of death, including Baude Fastoul, who wrote of his own suffering from advancing leprosy.[15] In the fifteenth century the 'Danse macabre,' or Dance of Death, became a feature of cemeteries, where it was depicted in painting on the walls; it appeared in a poetic version by Jean Gerson as well as in a *Danse macabre des femmes* attributed to Martial d'Auvergne.[16] François Villon focused on the prospect of his own death and the retrospective view it would grant him onto his friends and (especially) his enemies in this life. Villon's preliminary *Lais* ('Legacy') and his culminating *Testament* ('Last Will') represent a poet's lifework dedicated to anticipation of death.[17] In the 'Ballade

[15]See the poems called *Vers de la mort* by Robert le clerc d'Arras and Adam de la Halle, both in Jean-Marcel Paquette, ed., *Poèmes de la mort de Turold à Villon*, Collection 10/18 (Paris: Union Générale d'Édition, 1979). For the *congés* (poems of leavetaking), see Pierre Ruelle, ed., *Les congés d'Arras (Jean Bodel, Baude Fastoul et Adam de la Halle)* (Paris: Presses Universitaires de France, 1965). On Baude Fastoul, see Monique Santucci, 'Regards sur la vie dans les Vers sur la mort (Hélinand de Froidmont et Baude Fastoul),' *Hélinand de Froidmont (Colloque et exposition)*, Cahiers de l'Abbaye de St-Arnoult 2 (Warluis: A.D.A.M.A., 1987) pp. 45–54.

[16]See Paquette, *Poèmes de la mort*. Ann Tukey Harrison, ed., *The Danse Macabre of Women: Ms. fr. 995 of the Bibliothèque Nationale* (Kent, Ohio: Kent State University Press, 1994). Christine Martineau-Génieys, *Le thème de la mort dans la poésie française de 1450 à 1550* (Paris: Champion, 1978).

[17]See Barbara N. Sargent-Baur, ed., *François Villon: Complete Poems* (Toronto: University of Toronto Press, 1994).

des pendus' ('Ballad of the Hanged'), known also as his 'Epitaphe', Villon projected the speaker's point of view into the rotting corpse of a hanged man, dangling from the gibbet among several others:

> La pluye nous a debuez et lavez
> Et le soulail deceschez et noirciz.
> Pies, corbeaux nous ont les yeulx cavez
> Et arаché la barbe et les sourcilz.
> Jamais nul temps nous ne sommes assis;
> Puis ça, puis la, comme le vent varie,
> A son plaisir sans cesse nous charie,
> Plus becquetés d'oiseaux que dez a couldre. . . .
>
> The rain has soaked us and washed us clean
> And the sun dried us up and turned us black.
> Magpies and crows have hollowed out our eyes
> And plucked away our beards and eyebrows too.
> Never at any time are we at rest;
> This way and that, as the wind may vary,
> It pushes us about just as it likes,
> More pecked by birds than any sewing thimble. . . . [18]

This macabre depiction of the death of the body, deprived of all dignity, helps us realize the lengths to which Helinand did not go.

II
Medieval Literature of Bereavement

Of the several ways medieval literature treats the theme of death, the easiest for us to approach is perhaps the literature of bereavement.[19] Here the point of view is that of this world: death is undoubtedly bad, and feelings at the loss of a loved one range from grief to anger. Expanding our view beyond the immediate field of literature in French, we find expressions of bereavement for the loss of loved ones in many

[18] From the 'Ballade des pendus,' ed. Sargent-Baur, pp. 266–67.

[19] Literature of bereavement corresponds in general to the *planctus*, or lament. See D. Anselm Hoste, 'Aelred of Rievaulx and the Monastic Planctus,' *Cîteaux: Commentarii Cistercienses* 18 (1967) 385–98, on the traditions culminating in Aelred's lament for his friend Simon, written in 1142–43.

relationships to the speaker. The parents of Saint Alexis grieved for their son, as we have seen, the father in sadness and the mother in anger; in the *Song of Roland* Charlemagne grieved for his vassal Roland and took violent revenge. In the Old Occitan lyric *planh*, composed from the twelfth to the fourteenth century, the troubadour sang grief for a lord or a beloved lady.[20] The grief of a widower for his wife motivated a german prose composition written by Johann von Tepl in 1401–1407, *Der Ackermann aus Böhmen*, which moves from initial anger toward consolation.[21] Grief for a daughter animated the beautiful fourteenth-century english *Pearl* poem.[22] Petrarch wrote in praise of his late mother.[23] About 1215 the Cistercian Thomas of Beverly, a monk of Froidmont, wrote of the holy life and death of his sister, Margaret of Jerusalem.[24] Grief for a beloved woman—or girl—inspired Dante's *Vita Nuova* and later the *Comedy*.

Despite the masculine cast of so much medieval expression, we also find an occasional expression of grief by a woman. Among the trobairitz, or women troubadours, Azalais de Porcairagues grieved for her cousin Raimbaut d'Aurenga (died 1173) and an anonymous woman grieved for her beloved, possibly her husband (circa 1350).[25] The widowed Christine de Pizan grieved inconsolably for the husband she lost in 1390.[26]

[20] On the *planh* see Patricia H. Stäblein, 'New Views on an Old Problem: The Dynamics of Death in the Planh', *Romance Philology* 35 (1981) 223–34.

[21] Keith Spalding, ed., *Johann von Tepl: Der Ackermann aus Böhmen* (Oxford: Blackwell, 1950).

[22] E. V. Gordon, ed., *Pearl* (Oxford: Clarendon Press, 1953). Translation in John Gardner, *The Complete Works of the Gawain-Poet* (Chicago: University of Chicago Press, 1965) 95–145.

[23] See Elena Giannarelli, 'Fra mondo classico e agiografia cristiana: il *Breve panegyricum defuncte matri* di Petrarca,' *Annali della Scuola Normale Superiore di Pisa*, 3rd ser., 9 (1979) 1099–1118.

[24] Paul Gerhardt Schmidt, ''Peregrinatio periculosa': Thomas von Froidmont über die Jerusalem-Fahrten seiner Schwester Margareta,' *Kontinuität und Wandel: Lateinische Poesie von Naevius bis Baudelaire, Franco Munari zum 65. Geburtstag* (Hildesheim: Weidmann, 1986) 461–85.

[25] Angelica Rieger, ed., *Trobairitz: Der Beitrag der Frau in der altokzitanischen höfischen Lyrik, Edition des Gesamtkorpus* (Tübingen: Niemeyer, 1991) 480–504 (Azalais de Porcairagues), 662–74 (the anonymous *planh*).

[26] William D. Paden, 'Christine de Pizan as a Reader of the Medieval Pastourelle,' *Conjunctures: Medieval Studies in Honor of Douglas Kelly*, ed. Keith Busby and Norris J. Lacy (Amsterdam: Rodopi, 1994) 387–405. For translations

Two texts of bereavement invite comparison with Helinand's *Verses on Death*: the *Coplas por la muerte de su padre* by Jorge Manrique, who died in 1479, and the sermon by Bernard of Clairvaux in which he describes the loss of his brother Gerard (circa 1140). Having just lost his father, Manrique offsets his grief by impersonal considerations of the universality and ineluctability of death, and then balances it against pride in his father's life.[27] He represents Death as a figure who came to one of the towns his father held, knocked on the door, and invited the dying man to come away. Making no resistance, he consented 'with a joyful, clear and pure will': 'y consiento en mi morir/ con voluntad plazentera/ clara y pura.' He prayed to Christ to pardon him and died surrounded by his wife, his sons (including the poet who speaks), his family and servants. 'Although his life has perished, his memory has left us sufficient consolation.'[28] That memory united great and famous deeds with the virtue for which he was loved.[29] The poet consoles himself in a deeply personal way by summoning up all the grounds for his filial affection. The emotional tone of the *Coplas*, so bathed in love, contrasts sharply with the outrage which drove Helinand.

No less a Cistercian than Saint Bernard expressed powerful grief for his brother Gerard, speaking with the authority of abbot to the monks of Clairvaux, his spiritual sons, in the twenty-sixth of his *Sermons on the Song of Songs*. Bernard interrupts his commentary on the biblical text, overwhelmed by the sorrow which he has attempted to repress but which now, he realizes, is turning bitter.[30] The tension between his grief and his faith in a loving God drives him to confess his humanity, to admit his carnality:

---

see Renate Blumenfeld-Kosinski, ed., *The Selected Writings of Christine de Pizan* (New York: Norton, 1997).

[27]Text with English translation in J. M. Cohen, ed., *The Penguin Book of Spanish Verse*, 3rd ed. (London: Penguin, 1988) 48–75. Augusto Cortina, ed., *Jorge Manrique: Cancionero* (Madrid: Ediciones de La Lectura, 1929).

[28]Cohen, *Penguin Book of Spanish Verse*, pp. 72–75.

[29]Pp. 64–65.

[30]SC 26.II.3: 'At suppressus dolor altius introrsum radicavit, eo, ut sentio, acerbior factus, quo non est exire permissus'; J. Leclercq, C. H. Talbot, and H. M. Rochais, eds., *S. Bernardi Opera*, I: *Sermones super Cantica Canticorum 1–35* (Rome: Editiones Cistercienses, 1957) pp. 169–81, p. 171.

> Carnalem quis dixerit? Ego humanum non nego, sicut nec me hominem. Si ne hoc sufficit, nec carnalem negaverim. Nam et ego carnalis sum, venumdatus sub peccato, addictus morti, poenis et aerumnis obnoxius. Non sum, fateor, insensibilis ad poenas: mortem horreo meam et meorum. Meus Girardus erat, meus plane. An non meus, qui frater sanguine fuit, professione filius, sollicitudine pater, consors spiritu, intimus affectu? Is recessit a me: sentio, laesus sum, et graviter.[31]

> Will you say then that this is carnal? That it is human, yes, since I am a man. If this does not satisfy you then I am carnal. Yes, I am carnal, sold under sin, destined to die, subject to penalties and sufferings. I am certainly not insensible to pain; to think that I shall die, that those who are mine will die, fills me with dread. And Gerard was mine, so utterly mine. Was he not mine who was a brother to me by blood, a son by religious profession, a father by his solicitude, my comrade on the spiritual highway, my bosom friend in love? And it is he who has gone from me. I feel it, the wound is deep.[32]

'Mortem horreo meam et meorum': Gerard was Bernard's, and Bernard feels a staggering loss. This piercingly intimate confession jibes uneasily with the faith he is charged to sustain before his sons. He remembers that when death was near Gerard sang a psalm of praise, 'exulting in the hour of death, . . . his face lit up with joy.'[33] Weeping, Bernard concludes, is a sign, not of lack of faith, but of the human condition. He praises God's goodness to Gerard and his justice to the sinful Bernard. 'Have I not been completely fair when I said that the one who was punished deserved it, and the one who was crowned was worthy of it?'[34] Thus Bernard saves his faith in a loving God by proposing his own sinfulness as the justification of Gerard's death.

[31] SC 26.VI.9; SBOp 1:177.

[32] SC 26. VI.9; translated Kilian Walsh, *Bernard of Clairvaux: On the Song of Songs, 2,* CF 7 (Kalamazoo: Cisterican Publications, 1976) 58–73; here page 69.

[33] SC 26.VII.11; SBOp 1: 178–179; CF 7:70–71; Gerard sang Psalm 148, 'Praise ye the Lord from the heavens: praise ye him in the high places' (Douai). 'In morte exsultantem, . . . exhilarata quidem facie'.

[34] SC 26.VIII.13; SBOp 1:180; CF 7:72:'Punitus est qui debuit, et coronatus qui meruit'.

God is good, but evil enters the world because of evil man, as in the story of Adam. The lucidity of this solution escaped Helinand, whose complaints against ecclesiastical abuses find no satisfactory explanation and imperil his sense of divine justice.

Helinand does not grieve for anyone. Rather he instructs Death to visit those dearest to him: Bernard and Renaut, apparently uncle and nephew, otherwise unknown (stanzas 6 and 8); the villages of Pronleroy, Péronne, and Angivillers, all within a few kilometers north-east of Froidmont (stanzas 6 and 10); Philippe de Dreux, bishop of Beauvais, 'whom I love so' ('cui je aim tant', stanza 16, line 2); three men of power and position, the *Tibaudois* (stanza 18, line 5) or descendents of Thibaut, count of Champagne, whom he calls his friends ('mes amis', stanza 18, line 8). These powerful men were all involved in the scandal over Ingeburga, whom Philip Augustus of France repudiated unjustly. Perhaps Helinand reproaches them all for their part in this sinful deed.[35] We do not know of specific sins committed by the villagers of those three small places, or by the unknown Bernard and Renaut, but there is no doubt that Helinand considered them sinners. A rigorous moralist, he sends Death to them to deter them from sin.

III
Literature of Salvation

At the opposite extreme, in the literature of salvation death is seen as an instrument in the plan of a loving deity, and so, however painful the bereavement it may bring, it is undoubtedly a good thing.[36] In the prologue to the *Exordium Parvum*, the founders of the Cistercian Order expressed the wish that their successors in the Order, 'after having put off the burden of the flesh, might rest happily in perpetual

[35]See Paden, '*De Monachis rithmos facientibus*: Helinand de Froidmont, Bertran de Born, and the Cistercian General Chapter of 1199' (note 3 above).

[36]The theme of death seen in the light of salvation typifies the *consolatio*, on which see Peter von Moos, *Consolatio: Studien zur mittellateinischen Trostliteratur über den Tod und zum Problem der christlichen Trauer*, 4 vols. (München: Fink, 1971–72).

peace'.[37] In the *Life of Saint Alexis*, the crowd of the faithful rejoiced in the death of the saint who they knew would now intercede for them. Saint Francis, at about the time of his own death in 1226, praised the 'Altissimu, onnipotente, bon Signore' for providing the sun, the moon, and the stars; for providing wind, water, fire, and earth; for providing those who suffer and pardon; and finally, for providing 'sora nostra morte corporale,' 'sister our bodily death,' since they are blessed whom death will find living according to the Lord's most holy will.[38] Hugh, abbot of Marchiennes, who died in 1158, exemplified the blessing of such a death: 'When he was about to pass away he did not appear with wild eye and foaming mouth, as has befallen many, but as though drawing out and sending forth his spirit, as though exulting to go forth, like one who truly desired to be released and to be with Christ.'[39]

In the *Verses on Death* this sense of joyful death, of reunion with God, is difficult to find. If death provides anything like joy, it is perhaps the vengeful glee of the satirist who dispatches death to terrify wrongdoers within and without the church.

IV
Literature of Punishment and Reward

The Psalmist recognized the polarity of death I have been discussing. For David the death of a saint is precious: 'Pretiosa in conspectu Domini mors sanctorum ejus' ('Precious in the sight of the Lord is the death of his saints').[40] But the death of a sinner is the worst

[37]'Nos cistercienses, primi huius ecclesiae fundatores, successoribus nostris stilo praesenti notificamus . . . ut . . . quatinus deposita carnis sarcina, in requie sempiterna feliciter pausent': *Cîteaux: documents primitifs*, ed. François de Place and others (Cîteaux: Commentarii Cistercienses, 1988) p. 24.

[38]George R. Kay, ed., *The Penguin Book of Italian Verse* (Harmondsworth: Penguin, 1958) 1–2.

[39]'Non torvo oculo, non ore spumanti, ut multis evenit apparuit cum transiret, sed tantum spiritum extrahens & emittens quasi exire gestiens, sicut qui revera cupiebat dissolvi & cum Christo esse': Edmundus Martène and Ursinus Durand, *Thesaurus Novus Anecdotorum* (Paris: Delaulne, 1717, rpt. Farnborough: Gregg, 1968–69) volume 3: p. 1735. Platelle, 'La mort précieuse,' p. 170.

[40]Psalm 115:15, Douai translation. See Platelle, 'La mort précieuse,' p. 151.

misfortune: 'Mors peccatorum pessima' ('The death of the wicked is very evil').[41] For Helinand too, death was sweet to the good but bitter to the bad.[42]

In the *Divine Comedy* death is a reason for the blessed to rejoice, but terrible for the sinful. The distinction between innocence and guilt is doubled by a judgmental distinction between pity and severity. In *Inferno* Dante the pilgrim is continually torn between pity for the human suffering of the damned and severity for their offenses. This is the 'war of pity,' the *guerra . . . de la pietate* (2. 4–5), which pits the pilgrim's human sympathy against his faith in divine justice. Time and time again Dante shows pity for the suffering of damned souls, despite the scolding of Virgil, his rational guide. When he shows severity toward the shade of Filippo Argenti, in the circle of the wrathful, by cursing him to stay mired in tears and filth, Virgil embraces him, kisses him on the face, and hails him as an 'indignant soul,' adding that 'blessed is she who bore you' (8.44–45). But the pilgrim's momentary participation in the spirit of divine punishment does not last; only when he approaches the lowest realms of hell does he again treat the sinners he encounters with the same or greater severity. When Dante yanks hair out of the scalp of Bocca degli Abbati, a traitor to his country, another soul mistakes Dante for a devil (32.108), one of the devils whose task it is to persecute the damned. A devil Dante is not, but the devils in hell are servants of divine justice. A believer in that justice must grant his approval for their mission. The tension between pity and severity, between humanity and divinity, replicates the contrast between the attitudes that death is bad or good that we have traced in other works.

The result becomes convoluted in Dante's encounter with Brunetto Latini, whom Dante identifies as his own dear teacher, the man who taught him how one may gain eternity—but who has himself lost eternity in Dante's poem, because Dante the poet damns him for the sin of sodomy. While we have no trace of other evidence that Brunetto had this vice, Dante the poet, if he knew that his dear teacher was guilty of it, used that knowledge to damn him in the eyes

41 Psalm 33:22, Douai.

42 'Morz, douce as bons, as maus amere' (stanza 23, line 1).

of generations of readers. Thus severity and pity are joined in what has been called 'infernal irony.'[43]

The *Verses on Death* can be seen as similar to the *Comedy*, though much less fully developed. Helinand's impulse to punish wrongdoers with divine sanction represents potentially the same concept as Dante's. Like Dante the severe pilgrim, Helinand sends Death to his friends. Seen in this light, though, the *Verses on Death* correspond principally to *Inferno*, only fleetingly to *Purgatorio*, and very little to *Paradiso*. Helinand does not dispatch Death to visit anyone whom he regards as already saved.

V
Mors Suspecta

The Rule of Benedict provides, in the fourth chapter, a list of 'tools of good works'. After three maxims on eternal life and before a long series of recommendations on attitudes to take during life on earth, the Rule gives this principle regarding the point of transition, which is death: 'Mortem cotidie ante oculos suspectam habere' (4:47). This statement has been translated by the monks of Glenstal Abbey rather freely as 'To look death daily in the eye'.[44] The crux of the translation is 'suspectam,' literally 'mistrusted, suspected, that excites suspicion.'[45] Literally, then, the rule means 'To have death, that excites suspicion, daily before one's eyes.' Adalbert de Vogüé has explained the key term in this context as 'soupçonnée de vouloir survenir le jour même,'[46] that is, 'imminent, threatening'. As an instrument of good works the monk must daily think of

[43] John Freccero in *The Inferno of Dante*, trans. Robert Pinsky (New York: Noonday Press, 1994) 327.

[44] *The Rule of Benedict*, trans. Monks of Glenstal Abbey (Dublin: Four Courts Press, 1994).

[45] Charlton T. Lewis and Charles Short, *A Latin Dictionary* (Oxford: Clarendon Press, 1879).

[46] Adalbert de Vogüé, 'Avoir la mort devant les yeux chaque jour comme un événement imminent,' *Collectanea Cisterciensia* 48 (1986) 267–78, at p. 275. See also Sophie Hasquenoph, 'La mort du moine au Moyen Age (Xe-XIIe siècles),' *Collectanea Cisterciensia* 53 (1991) 215–32, especially pp. 219–21.

death as though it were imminent, because the thought of death will keep him from sin. Thus Ecclesiasticus: 'In omnibus operibus tuis memorare novissima tua, et in aeternum non peccabis'; 'In all thy works remember thy last end, and thou shalt never sin'.[47] Ser Lapo Mazzei quoted language from *Purgatorio* which expresses the same thought in other language: 'This whole life of ours is but a race towards death.'[48]

In the *Verses* Helinand holds death before the eyes of sinners to remind them that they must change their ways. The poem is 'an alarm-bell alerting the living to the constant presence of death,'[49] and as such falls squarely within monastic tradition, which used death without morbidity as an instrument for the understanding of life.[50] It is exceptional in that tradition because it is written in French, no doubt because it is directed to members of secular orders and lay society instead of monks. Helinand calls on bishops, kings, and commoners to honor this principle of the Benedictine Rule.

The poem is exceptional, too, because in extending the provision of the Rule to all of society, Helinand loses the positive and confident attitude toward death expressed by the Rule and instead sounds a more anxious note.[51] We return to the ambivalence we have traced throughout these remarks. As a monk, Helinand was drawn to see death as good, but as an ordinary man, a mere creature, he must

[47] Ecclesiasticus 7:40; for commentary see Adalbert de Vogüé, "'Memorare novissima tua': Sur la pensée de la mort chez saint Bernard et ses devanciers,' *Collectanea Cisterciensia* 52 (1990) 54–65.

[48] '. . . Se vivere si chiama quello che Dante dice, che è uno correre alla morte': Guasti, ed., *Lettere di un notaro*, volume 1:310. Trans. Origo, *The Merchant of Prato*, p. 341. Ser Lapo echoes 'vivi/ del viver ch'è un correre a la morte' (*Purgatorio* 33: 54); cf. 'Currite dum lumen vitae habetis, ne tenebrae mortis vos conprehendant' (Rule of Benedict, Prologue, 13); John 12:35.

[49] 'Un tocsin alertant les vivants de la présence constante de la mort': Emile Lanc, 'L'adaptation scénique des Vers de la mort', in *Hélinand de Froidmont (Colloque et exposition)* 75–85, at p. 77.

[50] 'Death-awareness is, precisely, a comprehension beyond all analogy that *death is*, which makes possible the comprehension that *life is*': A. W. Richard Sipe, 'Memento Mori: Memento Vivere—In the *Rule* of St. Benedict', *American Benedictine Review* 25 (1974) 96- 107, at p. 99.

[51] On the anxious note concerning death in monastic texts including the Rule, see de Vogüé, 'Avoir la mort devant les yeux chaque jour comme un événement imminent,' 277.

have been tempted to see it as bad. In addressing society beyond the monastery, he employed the fear of death as a rhetorical instrument to drive home his call to cease sinning, but the tone of his call reveals that he must have felt himself the fear he evoked. In the general design of the *Verses* death is an instrument of good works, an instrument created by a loving God; but in the tone of the poem death is frightful. The poem occupies the intersection of other-world and this world, of the divine and the human, of death as an instrument of divine love and death as an object of human fear. Small wonder we sense a shifting ambivalence in its tone.

A Commentary on The Fifty Stanzas of Helinand's *Verses on Death*

by Jenny Lind Porter

STANZA I Helinand, monk of Froidmont (1160–1229), composed his *Verses on Death* sometime between 1194 and 1197. In Stanza I the poet tells us that Death has caged him like a bird or, and the image shifts, made him like someone who, as if through hot baths, sweats to get rid of all toxins. The wise fear death, he writes, yet few are willing to change their habits and shed their skins. Whether we amble or run, we are all heading for Death. Helinand himself has undergone a change of heart; he has abandoned a frivolous life. The change is recent; his skin is yet moist with the exudant toxins.

Why does the poet say that Death has been the cause of his changed life? Perhaps a parent, a beloved friend, or a sweetheart died. Perhaps he barely escaped Death in a duel, in an accident, or in illness. Whatever it was, this revelation of Death's power came as a shock, and he wants others to understand the omnipotence of Death. This leads us to ask, where do we find Helinand as the poem opens, and where had he been before he made his momentous decision?

THE LIFE OF HELINAND

Helinand was born *c.* 1160, ninety-four years after William the Conqueror prevailed at the Battle of Hastings. In a latin work Helinand explains that his father, Hermann, and his uncle, Ellebaut, came to France from Flanders after the assassination of Charles the

Good (1127), when many noblemen feared reprisals even if they had not been implicated in any plot. Ellebaut became *cubicularius* (a chamberlain, an attendant on a lord) to Henry of France, the brother of King Louis VII and archbishop of Rheims from 1162–1175.

Helinand grew up as a member of the aristocracy. Through his family he moved in circles of power and prestige with friends who were the grand *seigneurs* and prelates of his day. Probably a native of Angivilliers, in the Oise, he early displayed an affinity for literature, both sacred and classical. His teacher in Beauvais was Raoul, a pupil of Peter Abelard.

By the time he was between twenty and twenty-five, he had become a *cointe damoisel*, an elegant courtier, as well as a noted *trouvère*, a minstrel. He lifted a goblet of wine at table, he rode in the hunt, he frequented theatres, and he was even called upon to perform before King Philip Augustus. The gallant young *trouvère* in his gold-embroidered mantle and furs, a stringed instrument in his hands, reciting some excerpt from the *chansons de geste*, must have been a dazzling sight in the court of the french king. His uncle Ellebaut and Henry of France no doubt listened with great pride to a performance which combined music, poetry, skilled oratory, and erudition.

In Paris Helinand would have seen the façade of the cathedral of Notre Dame, begun in 1163, the market at Les Halles, and the cathedral schools from which the University of Paris sprang. He said that he was a bird born to fly. After a few years of this life, the bird flew. It flew into the cistercian monastery at Froidmont, near Beauvais, and there Helinand remained for forty-four years. At about the age of thirty-five, when he had been a Cistercian for some ten years, Helinand wrote *Les Vers de la Mort*, translated into English as *Verses on Death*.

The meaning of Stanza I is now clear. The bird, the *trouvère*, has been caged. The fun-loving poet has become a cloistered monk. His life thus divides into two periods, the secular and the sacred. In the seventeenth century the English poet John Donne experienced a similar conversion and, dissatisfied with his worldly youth, moved on to write his famous sermons and Holy Sonnets and to become in 1621 the Dean of Saint Paul's Cathedral. Helinand lived to be about seventy, quite old for the time, and we have no reason to believe that he ever regretted his conversion.

HELINAND'S USE OF ALLITERATION

The alliteration which plays a vital part in Helinand's poem shows up in the first line: *Morz, qui m'as mis muer en mue.* It might be translated *Death, who immured me, molting new*, but the cage image should be retained even at the expense of some of the alliteration.

HELINAND'S STANZA FORM

The poem is long, containing six hundred lines composed of fifty stanzas of twelve lines each. Wulff and Walberg, in their critical edition of *Les Vers de la Mort*, call the stanza *La strophe de douze vers octosyllabiques distribués ainsi sur deux rimes*,[1] that is, a stanza of twelve octosyllabic lines with only two rhyme sounds.

Did Helinand invent the stanza form? Wulff and Walberg believe he did, although one Barthélemy, the 'Recluse of Molliens' (*c.* 1160–1230), also employed it and contributed to its popularity. Helinand's poem was widely imitated. Whether the stanza originated with him or not, Helinand handled it with consummate artistry, varying the caesura, offsetting the incessant sound of the two rhymes by run-on lines, and using dialogue and exclamations to loosen the formality of the verse. The translator must try to preserve as much of Helinand's technique as possible without departing from the main purpose, fidelity to the author's meaning. To the modern reader, the rhymes may create an excess of melody, but this is a medieval poem, and Helinand the *trouvère* well knew the mnemonic value of rhyme and alliteration.

[1] Fredrik Wulff and Emmanuel Walberg, *Les Vers de la Mort par Hélinant, moine de Froidmont, publiés d'après tous les manuscrits connus* (Paris: Librairie de Firmin Didot et Cie, 1905) XXVII.

STANZA II

Stanza II begins as Helinand salutes his friends, to whom Death is dispatched with urgent warnings that they must turn to God and prepare to face him after encountering Death. He first addresses his old friends, the *trouvères* and goliards of France. Teach them how to sing a new song, he writes; a sacred song instinct with spiritual awareness, a song which will bewitch and enchant even Death himself. If fear of God and love of God bear fruit in our lives, we are like mature trees which cannot easily be uprooted.

Note the many references in this poem to Death as a sorcerer, a wizard who enchants and uses spells.

HELINAND THE TROUVÈRE

The chants and hymns familiar to Helinand at Froidmont were unlike the songs he had known and performed as a *trouvère*. In addition to the *ballade* and the *lai*, the *trouvères* of northern France were accustomed to presenting *chansons de geste*, songs of heroic deeds. In court Helinand might have begun with a dramatic chord and the invocation, *Sing*, *O Muse*! and then have gone on to tell the tale of Dido and Aeneas. Now, in essence, he begins with *Sing*, *O trouvères*, *of a different kind of love*, *a different kind of sovereign*.

The *chansons de geste* Helinand knew may have centered around Charlemagne, King Arthur and his knights, or Troy. Although King Arthur had lived in Wales and southwestern England, the oldest cycle about his knights and their quest for the Holy Grail had been composed by Chrétien de Troyes (1140–1191), a *trouvère* attached to the court of Marie de Champagne at Troyes. It was Chrétien who wrote the famous *Perceval le Gallois*.

In the middle of the twelfth century a *trouvère* named Benôit de Sainte-Maure wrote the *Roman de Troie*, a long narrative poem about Troy which included a new theme: the love story of Troilus and Cressida. A century later Guido delle Colonne added Benôit's love story to his *Historia Trojana*. Benôit and Guido are thus the sources of Boccaccio's *Filostrato* (c. 1338), Chaucer's *Troilus and Criseyde* (1382–1385), which derived its plot from Boccaccio, and

Shakespeare's *Troilus and Cressida* (1601–1602). The fame of young Helinand and his memorable performance at court is alluded to by the *trouvères* Lambert li Tors and Alexander of Bernay in the *Roman d'Alixandre*:

> Quant li rois ot mangié, s'apiela Élinant
> Pour lui esbanoier li commande que cant . . .
>
> When the King [Alexander] had eaten, he called Élinant
> [Helinand] to entertain him and commanded him to sing.[2]

Technique

Stanza II is rich in assonance and resembles a liturgical chant in its cadence: *chanter*, *enchanter*. Helinand, long familiar with cistercian liturgy, would certainly have understood the power of the chants and the well-being conferred by certain combinations of tones. Were they enough to enchant Death, too?

Appeal to the Senses

The poem Helinand created is as austere and spare as cistercian architecture. In their simple and strong romanesque buildings, the Cistercians avoided statues, wall paintings, and stained glass, although later they would add gothic elements. A similar aesthetic governs Helinand's *Verses on Death*, where the only colors mentioned are silver, gold, and purple.

There is some appeal to the sense of taste: ham, bacon, cakes, bread (XLII); sizzling meat (XXIV); five kinds of fish (XLVII); beets and peas or *porée*, vegetable soup made with leeks (L). At the same time, we find little appeal to the sense of smell: smoke (XLII) and perfumed oil (XXV); and only limited appeal to the sense of touch: mud (III), downy beds (XXXVII), and thistles (XIV). Appeal to the eye is much greater, and there are visual images which linger in the mind: the bird in the cage (I); Death sharpening his razor (X);

[2] Wulff and Walberg, XVIII. The english translation is mine.

the poor fools sitting in the willow trees (XII); Death capering on the mound of a new victim (XXII); and the tarantula (XXV).

It is in his appeal to the sense of hearing that Helinand excels. A master of onomatopoeia, he lets us hear the songs of the abbey (II); Death's trumpet (VI); rats gnawing and nibbling (XIII); the clatter of horses' hooves (XIV); the click of dice (XV); the curses of the gambler (XV); the laughter of the insouciant young (XV); stones being hurled from a catapult (XXII); sizzling meat (XXIV); and the cyclonic winds (XLI).

When we remember that Helinand had spent a decade in the silence before he wrote this poem, we can understand how acute his sense of hearing and his sensitivity to sounds had become.

STANZA III In Stanzas III, IV, and V, Helinand sends Death to his friends with the serious message which lies at the heart of his poem. While there is yet time, they must turn away from worldliness. He addresses Death as you *who have the whole earth for rent* and sustains this address through ten lines until giving command. *I would salute my friends by* (*sending*) *you to put the fear of God into them.*

Line 10, with its reference to the mud in which people may sink, could well reflect Helinand's memories of Paris. The king during most of the poet's lifetime was Philip Augustus (ruled from 1180–1223), who became so exasperated with the stench of muddy parisian streets that he extravagantly decreed they should all be paved with solid stone. Long years later, thinking of how death can make *clever men slide clumsily*, Helinand may have gone back in his mind to the sight of elegant *seigneurs* slipping in the mud.

STANZA IV Having taken charge of his own misdirected energies, Helinand prays for his friends and explains that he has made vows which he believes include sharing his vision of life with them. The threats of Death may be salutary, causing young hedonists to reform.

STANZA V For you, Death, I have no love, says the poet, but I love the friends to whom I send you. I do not send you to harass and frighten but to comfort and guide them. You have brought us all to a frozen lake where mortals slip and slide. Anyone who sees his soul tightly bound and feels your arms encircling him is a fool if he does not repent. Notice the hissing sibilants which convey the sound of slipping and sliding.

STANZA VI The first five stanzas include one introductory stanza, one stanza directed to *trouvères*, and three stanzas addressed to friends, none of whom is named. In Stanza VI, for the first time Helinand uses the name of a close friend, Bernard. Stanza VI, VII, VIII, and IX form a unit. Two address Bernard (who came from Proneroi, now Pronleroy in Beauvais), and two address his uncle Renaut (who lived in Peronne). Bernard is contemplating monastic life but vacillating. Through his emissary Death, Helinand reminds Bernard that dallying until God's thunders stun may leave him forever outside paradise. The last two lines refer to a playful test of strength, *jeu de boute en courroie*. The young Bernard would have been familiar with this game, where two opponents tug mightily at each other's belt.[3] Each holds the buckle of his own belt but knows that if he loses, he is said to be outside paradise, unbuckled and unbound. The buckle represents security and, by analogy, the way in which faith holds us together.

STANZA VII Helinand sends Death to Bernard again, this time with sighs and tears. Here Bernard symbolizes every young person who finds it hard to leave old ways and choose the road less traveled by. With three questions Helinand heightens the drama. Why comes he not? Why long demur? Why late to merit such regard? If you wait too long, warns Helinand, you may get to the door and God will say, *Ne part ne hart*, Nothing doing.

STANZA VIII The poet then turns to Renaut, Bernard's uncle. His name provides a play on words: *Renaut . . . Re(g)ne en haut*, Reign on High. Helinand urges Renaut to protect himself through fear and love of God and to

[3]See Michel Boyer and Monique Santucci, *Hélinand de Froidmont, Les Vers de la Mort* (Paris: Librairie Honoré Champion, 1983) 111–112, Notes.

anticipate an arrow from Death's unfailing bow.[4] In line 9 Helinand pictures the soul at death crossing a river of glowing flames, likely an allusion to Phlegethon, the fiery river which formed one of the borders of Hades.

To complete his warning, the poet adds a biblical allusion. It is a poor carpenter who waits until his house is about to fall down before he attempts to fix the foundation. In the gospel according to Luke 6:47–49, Christ warns: *Whoever comes to me, and hears my sayings, and does them, I will show you who he is like. He is like a man who built a house, and dug deep, and laid the foundation on a rock: and when the flood arose, the stream beat vehemently upon that house, and could not shake it: for it was founded upon a rock. But he who hears, and does not act, is like a man who built a house without a foundation on the earth against which the stream beat vehemently, and immediately it fell and the ruin of that house was great.*

This stanza illustrates the commingling of classical and scriptural allusions in Helinand's *Verses on Death*. Indeed, Stanza VIII combines the three intellectual worlds of the poet: French literature, classical literature, and Scripture.

STANZA IX Stanza IX begins with a biblical allusion. Death, tell both uncle and nephew that the needle's eye lets pass very little of what we acquire on earth. In Mark 10:25 we read that *It is easier for a camel to go through the eye of a needle than for a rich man to enter into the kingdom of God.* Bernard and his uncle were doubtless men of property and wealth, and Helinand wanted them to consider the plight of the miser, who cannot really own anything, although he always wants more. *Qu'en avoir n'a point de savoir.* When avarice and wisdom try to work together, a third party always shows up, the devil. Line 9 offers a variation on the idea that when one speaks of the devil, he comes. The person who cheats death is the person who has only what he actually needs.

A brief look at the history of the Cistercian Order further clarifies Stanza IX.

[4] Wulff and Walberg, Notes, p. 51, attribute the expression *l'arc qui ne faut*, to the poet Béroul, referring to Tristan's bow.

HELINAND, THE CISTERCIAN

The Cistercian Order was founded in 1098 by Robert of Molesme and his companions, who sought to restore a strict observance of the benedictine rule. When Robert returned to his former monastery, Alberic and Stephen Harding succeeded him in turn. Like all Benedictines, the Cistercians took vows of obedience, stability, and conversion of life. The Cistercians treasured simplicity, celibacy, silence, and uniform discipline. These monks chose not to depend on feudal revenues and were willing to do menial tasks and hard labor, raising their own food and erecting their own structures if necessary.

Their vestments were simple; their meals frugal and vegetarian. In a latin work entitled *Liber de reparatione lapsi* or *Epistola ad Galterum* Helinand tells the story of a visit by Philippe de Dreux to the monastery. The bishop commented upon the glowing health of one young man, then asked:

> *Quid ergo comedisti hodie? Satis, inquit. Quid heri? Similiter satis. Non quaero, inquit, de quantitate sed de qualitate; quid comedisti heri, quid hodie? Heri, inquit, comedi pisa & olera, hodie olera & pisa: cras autem comedam pisa cum oleribus, postcras olera cum pisis.*[5]

> What therefore have you eaten today? he asked. Enough. And what yesterday? Just the same, enough. I do not ask, he said, about how much but the nature of what you ate yesterday and today. Yesterday, he replied, I ate peas and vegetable soup; today, vegetable soup and peas; tomorrow, on the other hand, I might eat peas with vegetables and the day after, vegetable soup with peas.

We assume that the young man was Helinand himself.

Cistercian buildings were in perfect harmony with the lifestyle of those who sought to identify with the lives of Christ's disciples. Saint Bernard (1090–1153) entered Cîteaux in 1113 and two years later led a quiet company of holy monks to a new monastery at

[5]Wulff and Walberg in their Introduction, XIX, XX cite Bertrand Tissier, *Bibliotheca Patrum Cistersiensium* (Bellefontaine, 1660–1669). The translation from the Latin is my own. Helinand does not mention his own name in this passage.

Clairvaux. Silence, prayer, little wine, no spices, no white bread, and lots of vegetables![6] When Bernard died in 1153, cistercian abbeys numbered 343. By the year 1300 there were 693 monasteries and 60,000 monks and uncounted nuns who followed the cistercian way. The order spread to England, to Spain, to Sweden, to Italy, and to the Holy Land.

Among these cistercian monasteries, the manuscripts of Helinand's *Verses on Death* were shared and copied. The abbey of Froidmont owned manuscripts of the poem in Helinand's own writing. In 1905 Wulff and Walberg published an edition which leaves all Helinand scholars in their debt. They compared all the extant manuscripts (twenty-four) which had survived the centuries, some of them in tatters, some only a few pages long. By painstakingly studying these survivors, Wulff and Walberg were able to produce a critical text now followed by scholars all over the world. It is the basis of the present translation into English verse. Even if Froidmont had not possessed the original manuscripts, attribution of the poem to Helinand would have been easy through internal evidence, for the friends mentioned in the poem were his friends, and the prelates he names were men he had known since childhood.

Against this background Stanza IX stands revealed as the sincere philosophy of a person who has come to understand the verse in the gospel of Saint Luke: *Take heed, and beware of covetousness: for man's life does not consist in the abundance of the things he possesses.*

STANZA X Again Helinand touches on how rapidly death may rob the rich of their acquisitions. This message is sent to his hometown of Angivilliers and ends with *Di moi a çaus d'Angiviler / Que tu fais t'aguille enfiler / Dont tu lor veus cosdre lor manches*. Death, writes Helinand, tell them you are threading your needle so you can sew up their sleeves. Monks often basted up the voluminous sleeves of their robes to keep them from getting soiled while they were cooking or gardening. Loosely

[6]See Bernard of Clairvaux: *Apologia* to Abbot William, translated by Michael Casey OCSO, in *Cistercians and Cluniacs: The* Apologia . . . , CF1A (Kalamazoo: Cistercian Publications, 1970).

basted sleeves could easily be returned to their original length. The inference is that his friends in Angiviler are getting their sleeves dirty in worldly affairs, but Death will be only too happy to stitch their sleeves up permanently. A subtle, quiet wit enlivens the *Verses on Death*.

STANZA XI Helinand makes a passionate plea to his friends, many still epicurean in their habits, to admit Christ into their hearts and lives. They say that they believe in God; let their lives show it. As the years passed, forty-four of them in the monastery, Helinand delivered many sermons, all in Latin, some preserved at Froidmont. One is identified as the last Helinand preached before his death. So eloquent and learned was he that when the old abbot died, Helinand was offered the honor of succeeding him. Helinand did not accept the offer.

DYNAMIC VERBS OF THE POEM

An examination of Helinand's vocabulary reveals that some one hundred seven dynamic verbs give the *Verses on Death* its energetic movement and quick tempo. He does not rely on commonplace verbs like *is*, *go*, *seem*. Helinand uses graphic verbs like *strip*, *slide*, *sink*, *glide*, *hound*, *prune*, *tantalize*, *stretch*, *hammer*, *gnaw*, *crawl*, *sift*, *leer*, *crouch*, *leap*, *shear*, *carve up*, *prick*, *rob*, *grip*, *squeeze*, *tease*, *dart*, *pamper*, *plunder*, *smother*, *skin*, *damn*, *curse*. Very often the verbs are onomatopoeic.

STANZA XII In this stanza, Helinand sends Death to princes who think nothing of stripping the poor of what little they have. He refers to Saint Martin of Tours (316–397), a patron saint of France and the father of monasticism in Gaul, who said, 'I am Christ's soldier'. Martin founded a community of hermits at Ligugé, which became the first monastery in Gaul and remains a benedictine abbey to this day.

Wulff and Walberg claim that Helinand evidently knew a story about the saint which, although it is noted in an hagiographic compilation, *Summa de vitis sanctorum*, is not contained in the two chief biographies of Saint Martin. Martin and his companions were cultivating the fields when *ecce subito torrens abundantissimus de montibus per prata descendens velut diluvium cuncta submergere et subvertere cepit*. A mountain torrent suddenly threatened to inundate the field. *Tunc sanctus, stans immobilis*, then the saint, unmoving and unafraid, called to the men to stay with him. Unfortunately, a number of them failed to heed him but ran off and climbed willow trees along the river bank. The branches bent, and the men were drowned. All those who stayed with Saint Martin were saved.[7] They should have depended on God, of course, and they would not have wound up pendent on the willow tree. Thus in Stanza XII Helinand warns princes about the consequences of placing too much faith in material things.

STANZA XIII Helinand sends Death to Rome and the church hierarchy. His attack on the worldiness of some prelates may have been the reason the poem was first published anonymously. He stood in a long traditiona which in later years included Dante and Chaucer. Both devout churchmen, they also satirized worldly clerics. In translation *Va moi saluer la grant Romme* becomes *Hail*, as in *Ave Roma immortalis*, the traditional salute to Rome. Helinand traced the etymology of Rome's name to the latin word *to gnaw*, *to eat up*, *to torment* and *nibble upon*, in Old French *rongier*, modern French *ronger*. This stanza comes alive through onomatopoeia: the drum-like *pomme*, *homme*, *Romme*, *nomme* suggest the pageantry of a papal procession while *os ronge* brings nibbling rats to mind. In English *gnaw* and *nibble*, *tooth* and *gum* give us a sense of the mastery of sound in the original, and the percussive sounds are fairly well preserved by *come*, *succumb*, *numb*.

The simony to which Helinand alludes refers to the buying or selling of such spiritual things as sacraments or benefices. The word was coined from the name of Simon Magus, a Samaritan magician who was willing to pay quite a sum if he could be taught how to impart the Holy Ghost by the laying on of hands (Acts 8:9–24). Simony became

[7] Wulff and Walberg, Notes, 52–53.

a symbol of ecclesiastical corruption in the late eleventh century gregorian reform movement.

Throughout the stanza we hear that Rome offers many things for sale. Even the pope's legate, ostensibly a star in the eyes of common people, is described as a poor candle which sheds a dim light. Helinand and all of France knew that William of Champagne, archbishop of Rheims (1176–1202) and papal legate, was the prelate who had declared Philip Augustus' second marriage, to Ingeborg of Denmark, null and void. About the time Helinand wrote his *Verses on Death*, the king had just married a third wife, Agnes of Merán. It was the scandal of the day.

STANZA XIV Stanza XIV is paired with Stanza XIII. Helinand delights in plays on words and has fun with the similarity between the words *chardon* (thistle) and *chardonal* (cardinal). These luxury-loving prelates desire gifts and a soft life; they avoid suffering and flee a crown of thorns like that which Jesus wore. The crown of thorns was fashioned from a thistle-like plant (*chardon*) which the cardinals (*chardonal*) shun. The cardinals are likened to dying coals, slugs and clinkers. They remind us of Chaucer's Monk who craved a fat swan, a thorough-bred horse, and a cloak with grey fur on its sleeves.

STANZA XV A reference to Rheims recalls Helinand's uncle Ellebaut, a chamberlain of Henry of France, who was archbishop of Rheims from 1162–1175. Philip Augustus had become the king of France in 1180. Nine years later, his first wife, Isabella, died. Later he married Ingeborg, princess of Denmark, in what was probably a political match. The king conceived an aversion to her after the first day and persuaded a council of french bishops to annul the marriage. Ingeborg was sent to a monastery, and in 1196 Philip married Agnes of Merán. When Pope Celestine II excommunicated him, Philip retorted that he would rather give up half his kingdom than give up Agnes. In the end, under pressure of Pope Innocent II's displeasure, Philip had to part with Agnes and in 1200 bring Ingeborg back to Paris. Philip tripled the size of french territories, built the Louvre as a fortress to guard the Seine, and encouraged the building of Notre Dame cathedral, but he never lived down the Ingeborg scandal.

Mention of Rheims also brings to mind William of Champagne, archbishop of Rheims and the king's uncle, who declared null and void the marriage of Philip Augustus and Ingeborg. All this lay behind Helinand's references to Rheims and Death's boast that he has Rome and Rheims in his hands, despite their power.

'Gird up your loins', Helinand writes in line 4, echoing the First Epistle of Peter 1:13: *Wherefore gird up the loins of your mind, be sober, and hope to the end for the grace that is to be brought to you at the revelation of Jesus Christ.* Or perhaps he was thinking of Luke 12:34: *Let your loins be girded about and your lights burning.*

STANZA XVI Helinand dispatches Death next to Beauvais, to Philip de Dreux, a bishop of that city who was imprisoned at Babylon during the Crusades and returned to France in 1193. Richard the Lion-Hearted threw de Dreux in prison again in 1197, to avenge himself on Philip de Dreux for his earlier intrigues aimed at keeping Richard himself in prison. The bishop did not regain his freedom until 1199. This same Philip de Dreux, it was said, was better suited to a helmet than a mitre. He was involved in all manner of political and religious intrigue, so it is small wonder that Helinand felt apprehensive about his friend, the bishop *who's always held me dear. Henceforth he must be vigilant.*

STANZA XVII The *bishops twin* mentioned here are two brothers, Philip de Dreux, the bishop of Beauvais (1176–1217) we just met, and his brother Henry, bishop of Orleans (1186–1198). They were cousins of the king and nephews of the archbishop of Rheims. The bishop of Noyon mentioned in Stanza XVII was Stephen of Nemours (1188–1221). All these bishops were friends of Helinand and his uncle Ellebaut.

STANZA XVIII Thibaut the Great, count of Champagne and Blois, had a number of descendants who were prominent in the France of Helinand's day. In saluting Chartres, Chalons, and Blois, the poet sends Death to three of Thibaut's grandsons: Count Louis of Blois (1172–1205); Renaut, bishop of Chartres from 1182–1217; and Rotrou, bishop of Chalons-sur-Marne from 1190–1200.

STANZA XIX Helinand sends his grim emissary to the prelates of Normandy, England and France. By 1066 England had known five conquerors: the Celts, the Romans, the Anglo- Saxons, the Danes and the Normans. Helinand uses the word *Englois*, derived like our words *English* and *England*, from *angle* or *engle*. Angles, Saxons, Jutes, and Frisians had invaded Britain when that land was called Britannia, a province of the Roman empire. After the Norman conquest, English, the speech of the descendants of these Angles and Saxons, became the language of a subjugated people. Latin and French became the languages of the cathedral, the law, the schools, and the court. English kings married French women and imported French prelates.

When the Cistercians spread to England, their services were chanted in Latin and their business with landowners was conducted in French. When Philip Augustus and Richard the Lion-Hearted went on the Third Crusade together, they spoke French to each other quite naturally.

Helinand's message in Stanza XIX presupposes this relationship between the two kingdoms and the rivalry between their two famous kings. Because of the Norman victory in 1066, England's king was the vassal of the French king. Yet England held more land in France than did its king, and in defense of these lands the English king had destroyed a number of churches. Philip retaliated by subjecting some of Richard's churches and priests to destruction and death. If we bear in mind that the French king had defied the pope in his marriage, the meaning of Stanza XIX is clear. The lay powers had both injured clerics and flouted the See of Rome, to say nothing of heavy taxes they had levied to finance the Crusades. Helinand may also have been thinking about the foully murdered and quickly canonized Thomas Becket at Canterbury.

Why does the Church not rise up against these rulers who believe they can pillage and murder in sacred communities with impunity? The Church has twin means to enforce its will: authority from God and eternal punishment. Helinand uses the word *cornes* (horns) to signify spiritual antennae, rays of light like those which medieval and renaissance artists depict on Moses. A long artistic convention also indicates authority and holiness by auras or aureoles around the heads of special persons.

STANZA XX With some diffidence Helinand addresses *ambesdeus les rois*, the two kings, Philip and Richard. Death is sent to remind them that he can easily unbeard them, that is, deprive them of their power. As a matter of fact, Richard the Lion-Hearted died in France in 1199, fatally wounded in a siege, three or four years after this poem was written. Stanza XX ends with an apt image for kings and nations plotting war. Death spreads a net before the kings. In the Bible we read of nets being hidden in the brush along a trail and sometimes covered with a thin layer of soil. The operator could pull the concealed net around the unsuspecting game which wandered or was driven into them. Psalm 140:5 reads, *The proud have hidden a snare for me. They have spread a net by the wayside: they have set a trap for me.* Stanzas V and XXXI employ this same image.

STANZA XXI Death is equally interested in king and peasant.

> Mors, tu abaz a un seul tor
> Aussi le roi dedenz sa tor
> Com li povre dedenz son toit.

Helinand may unconsciously have echoed Horace:

> Hold! Pale Death, at the poor man's shack
> and the pasha's palace kicking,
> Impartially announces his arrival.[8]

The stanza describes how Death summons each person to a final account for his debts. The soul may work to see that all accounts are settled before death, but she cannot pay debts in the way mortals do. She must pay through suffering.

[8] Horace, *Odes*, translated by James Michie, *The Oxford Book of Death* (Oxford: Oxford University Press, 1983) 9.

STANZA XXII Death has besieged the whole earth. He enjoys seeing an unlikely candidate for the grave suddenly faced with that very reality. The athleticism and cunning of Death, the warrior in this stanza, cannot be overcome in battle. Elsewhere in Helinand's *Verses*, Death is portrayed as a runner, a gambler, a hunter, a sorcerer, a debt-collector, a prankster, a thief, a thug, an equestrian, a voyeur, a musician, a barber, a sneak, a landlord, a tailor, a hostile witness, a judge, a cook, a sadist, a stalker, an archer, a traitor, an arbitrator, and a mischief-maker. He is quick, graceful, confident. He is everything but a fool, and he loves his work. Even though Helinand personifies death, the reader never loses the sense of Death as an eternal mystery. Only once, in Stanza XII, does Death enter with the traditional scythe.

STANZA XXIII Like the youthful Shakespeare, Helinand loved word plays. He also appreciated the element of contrast, as in Stanza XXIII, one of the most beautiful and poignant of the entire poem.

> The son precedes the father's bier,
> Flower is gathered ere the fruit,
> The body, an unbroken shoot,
> The soul that scarcely sinks her root,
> All stricken with a logic queer.

Helinand realized that many of his still young friends considered death a long way off—at their peril.

STANZA XXIV This, the most sensual of all Helinand's stanzas, is also, apart from Stanza I, the most clearly autobiographical. He had himself been one of these *cointes damoiseaux* to whom he refers, jolly and carefree, interested in women, hunting, wine, choice food, laughter, and song. The structure of the stanza is a carefully sustained parallel. The dandies go hunting, kill, and dress out the meat. They are burning to have the choicest morsels; they are eagerly anticipating the meal, and one can imagine them cavorting and singing as they listen to the pop and sizzle of the dripping pan. They pay homage to the meat, not to a *seigneur*. Then Death stalks, kills, and dresses out the jocund courtiers. The last line reads, *en plein miedi lor anuite*. In plain day darkness comes. The noonday darkens.

Lines 6–9 refer to *ces cointes damoisiaus*, plural, but because of the strictures of rhyme and meter, in the translation one dandy must stand for all.

Note Helinand's onomatopoeia in ll.6–7, where the words and the rhythm both suggest the sound of the horses' hooves, and in l.9, where *leschefrite* (dripping pan) has a popping sound, here expressed through the English word *sizzling*.

STANZA XXV The central idea of this stanza recalls Psalm 111:10: *The fear of the Lord is the beginning of wisdom*. Stanza XXV is directly tied to Stanza XXIV and the jaunty courtiers. Helinand observes that Death has our hands tied from the womb and may decide to take someone when he is no more than twenty-five or thirty, no matter how fancy his garments or sweet his perfume.

STANZA XXVI The holy soul has everything in order, and over that soul Death has no power. The sinful, unrepentant person is in trouble.

STANZA XXVII Helinand stresses the importance of early lessons in ethics and spirituality. They have taught us well who in our youth have given us something to cling to; over and over again we return to their words of wisdom. They provide food to us, nurturing the inner person. *Train up a child in the way he should go*, says Proverbs 22:6, *and when he is old, he will not depart from it*.

STANZA XXVIII Stanzas XXVIII and XXIX begin with questions. We spend years acquiring possessions. What good are they? Death, who never loses, will get them all. In the silence of the abbey, Helinand must often have smiled at the memory of the pompous, bombastic, garrulous, and glib *big talkers* he had known. Death silences them, even *les plus emparlez*, the habitual babblers. Death makes jokers weep and puts sackcloth and ashes on a level with purple raiment and fine ermine.

STANZA XXIX Again a question begins the stanza. What good are beauty, wealth, honors, rank? Death can do with them what he likes. He can bring rain or drought, and he seizes those whom he disprizes and those whom he prizes. Death likes to find a fat man with a soft stomach and then coat that stomach with fire and worms.

Note the easy, graceful rhythm and the varied pauses of Stanzas XXVIII and XXIX. The allusion to rain and drought in connection with Death seems to be linked to the disastrous floods and winds which ruined crops in the countryside around Beauvais in 1194 and caused many deaths by drowning.

STANZA XXX Death proves that the All we thought so important may in reality be Nothing. Note the alliteration in the Old French: all that gluttony can englut and all that lechery can leech. Death is never satisfied by a new victim; he is insatiable. At last Death says something: *tprot. Rot*!

STANZA XXXI The tone grows more sombre. Ten of the lines in this stanza begin with *Morz*, Death. Death gives the poor man what he lost / Death takes from the rich man everything he gained. Line 5 is an excellent example of Helinand's powers of condensation: Death provides *a muddy blanket for our nap*.

STANZA XXXII The driving rhythms of Stanzas XXXI, XXXII, and XXXIII depend on the almost total absence of the caesura and the use of the word *Morz* at the beginning of almost every line. This set of stanzas recounts what Death has done and may do. *Death gives the proud up to manure*. The phrase, *saveur de bon craspois*, translated here as *seasoning*, really means fat, lard, grease. Adding drippings or grease to vegetable soup would have imparted flavor, but despite a longstanding allowance of lard in european monastic diets (since 816 AD), the disciplined vegetarian Cistercians did not permit its use.

STANZA XXXIII This is the third stanza of the set defining the powers of Death. The French were constantly taxed to finance the Crusades, and those who could not go, paid. If the money were collected and the crusaders did not go, then they were false crusaders.

STANZA XXXIV Shame on those who have no fear of Death, says the poet. Shame, too, on those who worry all the time about when and how they may die. Line 4 contains one of Helinand's plays on words: *faillir sans faille*. We can't hold on to life indefinitely, for without fail we must fail—that is, die.

> For in this game he's impotent;
> He clings to something transient:
> Death shortens every long goodbye.

The last six lines of Stanza XXXIV are devoted to those who take a *carpe diem* attitude. Some never think about Death and have no fear of it, says the poet; some think about it all the time and dread it; and some say they don't have time to think about it and, anyway, why should they? *Let's just take the good that comes to us and afterward, let come what may. Death is the end of the battle of life when the soul and the body become nothing.*

STANZA XXXV Stanza XXXIV ended with the insouciance of *li fol*, the fools. Stanza XXXV immediately observes that some ancient philosophies held that there is no hereafter and no God. The Roman Epicureans thought we should live our lives in pleasure without fear of divine retribution. If this were true, the poet continues, we might as well live lives of debauchery rather than continence. If there were no heaven, then there would be no difference between the souls of man and pig.

STANZA XXXVI If there were no other *siècles*, no other cycles of life, then the body might indeed indulge itself on earth and do as it pleased. People would live like swine. And, Helinand wants to know, if there is no merit in virtue, what of the poor *ermite*, the hermits who deny themselves everything except bare essentials? Helinand speaks of monks who have downy beds (XXXVII), but the Cistercians slept on straw pallets. Are they mistaken in dedicating their lives to God and living humble, prayerful lives? Have they missed the boat?

STANZA XXXVII The Cistercians were aware that many abbeys had standards less strict than their own. There had been a heated exchange on the subject of observances early in the twelfth century, and Helinand echoes it when he speaks of monks who eat sweets and sleep on downy beds.

The procession referred to in line 5 satirizes the great pomp and ceremony of other orders. These Fat Craws may neglect their covenant with God, but they join processions to the refectory promptly enough.

STANZA XXVIII If God does not reward those who make sacrifices for him, then a fine-bred youth (like Helinand) who gives up great riches to enter the White Monks and who humbles himself before God behaves foolishly. The members of the Cistercian Order wore simple robes of unbleached wool. Hence they became known as the White Monks, members of the White Order (line 8). Was it all for nothing, muses Helinand?

Saint Lawrence (†258), one of the early christian martyrs, was a deacon of the Roman Church during the pontificate of Saint Sixtus I. The Emperor Valerian executed both the pope and Lawrence. But before he was arraigned, Lawrence had handed over the Church's treasures to the indigent and the sick. Bishop Ambrose of Milan and others attested to the fact that Lawrence was tortured by a savage method: roasted and grilled to death on a gridiron. He said to his persecutors, *I am cooked on that side; turn me over and eat.* If a person of integrity and goodness like Saint Lawrence receives *no* reward in heaven, then (ll. 10–12) he was indeed misled *qui fu rostiz et graeilliez / Et fist por Dieu de son cors haste.*

> Roasted and grilled till he was dead
> And turned upon the spit to baste.

Mass conversions are said to have followed, and even some Roman senators who saw what Valerian did to the saintly deacon, decided to become Christians. The Basilica di San Lorenzo now stands over his burial place.

STANZA XXXIX Stanza XXIX affirms the judgement of the saints and patriarchs that the good man and the evil man have a different lot in the afterlife. Helinand depicts princes and constables, representatives of power and law, seated at a table in heaven. It remains for us to attain that honor, as they did, by living lives of integrity. Compare to this Luke 22:29–30, *And I appoint unto you a kingdom . . . that you may eat and drink at my table in my kingdom, and sit on thrones*, or Matthew 8:11–12, *And I say to you, that many shall come from the east and west, and shall sit down with Abraham and Isaac and Jacob, in the kingdom of heaven.*

STANZA XL This begins a set of four stanzas which convey the compassion of the sensitive poet and gentle spiritual father for the humble folk of the earth, the hungry, the abused, those who suffer lack of food, medicine, and shelter. Some persons do not hesitate, he says, to skin the helpless wretches *whom the raw winds seek.* Helinand is repelled by man's inhumanity to man.

STANZA XLI Death, he writes, you employ your arms against those who tax and plunder; you torment those who ignore suffering, and yet they keep on doing it. Even the greatest *seigneurs* persist in this behavior. It is like a storm, a whirlwind which pushes souls from the right path. Once more Helinand seems to refer to the catastrophic floods and winds which affected the region of Beauvais in 1194.

STANZA XLII Now and then Helinand uses an exclamation to make his verse more natural. Here he inserts *Ha*! In Stanzas XLI and L he uses *Hé*! (*Ah* or *Oh*!) Death is busily in pursuit of the proud and selfish, writes Helinand, but the truth is, the more a man has, the more he wants. If he has a ham, he wants bacon; if he has cakes, he wants bread. The richer he is, the more he pinches pennies. *And colder is he, wrapped in plume.* Misers virtually consume a poor man's blood (l. 5). Many centuries later Charles Dickens created an immortal story around just such a person, Scrooge.

Notice the scratching sound of Death's nails (*ongles*), conveyed by the verbs in the *b* rhyme position: *fiches*, *triches*, *fliches*, *miches*, *riches*, *chiches*, all reminding us of the sound we hear when a sharp fingernail is drawn across a hard surface.

STANZA XLIII The last of the four stanzas on the exploitation of the poor and weak concludes that either there is no God or God will indeed sit in judgment on human deeds. Helinand believes with Matthew 13:49: *So shall it be at the end of the world: the angels shall come forth, and sever the wicked from among the just.* When the time comes, young and old together will issue forth from the trial of life, and Death will allow each soul to see *all records of its mortal race*, *toz ses biens et ses maus*, the good and the bad. Then each person shall realize the truth, that we must follow God's commandments, for life is not a place for jesting. For Helinand life is a test of character and a time for the growth and re-formation of a soul created in God's image and likeness and deformed by sin.

STANZA XLIV Stanza XLIV is the first of another group of four, this time the contrast is drawn between Saint Peter and the Emperor Nero. Nero Claudius Caesar ruled from AD 54–68. Cruel and dissipated, Nero perpetrated some incredible atrocities. He murdered his wife Octavia, his mother Agrippina, and the Emperor Claudius' son, Britannicus. His teacher, Seneca, resigned from court, but Nero made him commit suicide. He built a golden house, for which even Achaia and Asia were taxed. See Stanza XLVII, *He who so many golden bars. . . . Had robbed on either hand in greed.* When Rome burned in AD 64, Nero suspected or chose to blame the Christians and launched a persecution. Saint Paul and Saint Peter both met death at his command. Nero, sentenced to death after the Senate declared Galba emperor, fled and committed suicide on 9 June 68.

Helinand contrasts the extravagant comforts Nero demanded with the simple life of the apostle Peter, a fisherman from Bethsaida, a fishing village outside Capernaum on the Sea of Galilee.

STANZA XLV Helinand sustains the contrast between Nero and Saint Peter. Line 9 says that the wolf devoured the lamb, recalling Matthew 10:16, *Behold, I send you forth as sheep in the midst of wolves.*

STANZA XLVI Helinand reviews the promise of the Church to her faithful: *Be faithful to death and I will give you a crown of life*—Revelation 2:10. Helinand believed that justice would prevail. In Stanza XLIV he had written that Nero persecuted and murdered Peter, and we all with our own eyes have seen situations where it looked as if evil were going to triumph and as if the morally superior person were going to lose out.

For each has seen a paragon
By his inferior undone.

Yet we have also seen that good ultimately triumphs. One may reflect upon this, counsels Helinand, as he considers the plight of good Saint Peter in chains.

STANZA XLVII The last of the four stanzas on Saint Peter and Nero follows the musings of Stanza XLVI. The contrast between Nero and Peter is sharpened by our own knowledge that many Christians thought of Nero as the Anti-Christ,while Peter was elevated to sainthood and considered the rock on which Christ founded his Church.

STANZA XLVII has a tight structure: *He who* (1–3), *Who* (4–6), *Who* (7–8), *Who* (9), *Who* (10) . . . *Now* (11). The language is sensual, like the character of Nero. *He who* robbed; *who* ordered the finest meals; *who* wasted so much time on his body; *who* couldn't go anywhere without a thousand chariots; *who* never wanted to subject himself to God's will, *now* has to endure the fires of Hell. Helinand ends the stanza with a bit of sly humor, *And he is very warm who chars*. The fires of hell make an appropriate parallel to the fires of Rome.

STANZA XLVIII If the wicked are to have the same end as the virtuous, and if they may freely pass the bridge into the next world and be treated as good people are, then I'd say God doesn't mete out justice, writes Helinand. But that is not to be. All persons receive their just reward. *And many of them that sleep in the dust of the earth shall awake, some to everlasting life, and some to shame and everlasting contempt*, Daniel 12:2, reminds us.

STANZA XLIX Helinand returns to his central theme. We must all die and come to judgment. No one can prevent death, but everyone can prepare for it. We can repent of our sins and purge our imperfections. It is unwise to procrastinate. *The night is far spent*, Romans 13:12 warns us, *the day is at hand; let us therefore cast off the works of darkness and let us put on the armor of light.*

Lines 10–12 bring us the image of a boat sailing securely on the sea after its owner has caulked it well before leaving port.

STANZA L The six hundred-line poem draws to a close with lines reminiscent of a sigh. We picture Helinand at Froidmont, digging among the beets and peas of the abbey gardens, satisfied that this, his last poem, has turned his greatest talent to the service of God. *Pourquoi*? Why have men chased ephemera and carnal joys which corrupt our nature? Why are they willing to pay so dear a price for them? These worldly pleasures of ours are of short duration and often leave us bitter and restless.

The poem ends with a burst of energy. *Fui, lecherie*! *Fui, luxure*! Away, lechery! Away, luxury!

> Fie, gluttony and lust and lure,
> I gladly from your feast am poor
> Unto my beets and peas retired.

It was 1197, eight hundred years ago. Helinand was still a young man. He would remain at Froidmont the rest of his life, no longer the *trouvère* of King Philip Augustus but the humble and contented *serviteur* of the King of kings.

LES VERS DE LA MORT

VERSES ON DEATH

I

Morz, qui m'as mis muer en mue
En cele estuve o li cors sue
Ce qu'il fist el siecle d'outrage,
Tu lieves sor toz ta maçue,
Ne nus por ce sa pel ne mue
Ne ne change son viez usage.
Morz, toi suelent cremir li sage:
Or queurt chascuns a son damage:
Qui n'i puet avenir s'i rue.
Por ce ai changié mon corage
Et ai laissié et gieu et rage:
Mal se moille qui ne s'essue.

I

Death, who have caged me, molting new,
Cooped up where body sweats in rue
And pines excesses of the age,
You raise your mallet to man's view
But no one bids the past adieu
Nor sheds his habits' villeinage.
Death, you are feared by every sage,
Yet each advances to that wage,
Rambles or races, both will do.
Myself a change of heart engage,
I've left all play and badinage,
Shivering and soaked with undried dew.

II

Morz, va m'a çaus qui d'amors chantent
Et qui de vanité se vantent,
Si les apren si a chanter
Com font cil qui par ce t'enchantent
Que tot hors del siecle se plantent,
Que tu nes puisses sozplanter,
Morz, tu ne sés çaus enchanter
Qui le tien chant suelent chanter
Et la paor Dieu en enfantent:
Cuers qui tel fruit puet enfanter,
Por voir le puis acreanter
Que nul tien gieu ne le sozplantent.

II

Death, hie to those who sing love's chaunt
And who vainglories vainly flaunt
And teach them how to sing as they
Who for bewitching you are wont
To take themselves from worldly haunt
In shelter from your rude affray.
O Death, your spells cannot betray
Those folk who sing your roundelay
In all the fear of God, savant.
A heart which bears such fruit, I say
Won't be uprooted in dismay,
Can't be uprooted by your taunt.

III

Morz, qui en toz lieus as tes rentes,
Qui de toz marchiez as les ventes,
Qui les riches sés desnuer,
Qui les levez en haut adentes,
Qui les plus poissanz acraventes,
Qui les honeurs sés remuer,
Quil les plus forz fais tressuer
Et les plus cointes esluer,
Qui quiers les voies et les sentes
O l'en se seut empaluer:
Je vueil mes amis saluer
Par toi, que tu les espoentes.

III

Death, who have lots of ground to rent,
Who tax the least emolument,
Who strip the richest company,
Who bring to dust the eminent,
Who conquer the omnipotent,
Who change all fiefdoms by decree,
Who make the strong sweat generously
And clever men slide clumsily,
Who all the lanes and paths frequent
Where mud can sink us, cap-à-pie:
Go now to all my friends for me,
Give them this awesome testament.

IV

Morz, je t'envoi a mes amis,
Ne mie com a anemis
Ne com a gent que je point hace,
Ainz proi Dieu (qui el cuer m'a mis
Que ce li soille qu'ai pramis)
Qu'il lor doint longe vie, et grace
De bien vivre tot lor espace.
Mais tu qui gieues a la chace
De çaus o Dieus paor n'a mis,
Mout fais grant bien par ta menace,
Car ta paors purge et saace
L'ame aussi com par un tamis.

IV

Death, to my friends now go for me,
Not as it were to enemy
Nor as to persons whom I hate,
For I pray God (who set me free
To keep my promise faithfully)
Long life He give them and sweet fate
Of righteous living, long and late.
But you, who hunt the reprobate
In whom no godly fear must be,
Great good it is your threats create,
Because your siftings isolate
The soul in all its purity.

V

Morz, qui nos as toz pris al laz,
Qui en toz lieus fais verreglaz
Por nos faire verreglacier,
Certes, voirs est que je te haz,
Mais çaus o je t'envoi non faz,
Ainz le faz por aus solacier,
Por vanité loing d'aus chacier
Qui se poine d'aus portracier
Tant qu'aves les ait faiz o maz.
Mais qui te voit s'ame enlacier
De totes parz et embracier
Fous est s'il ne lest ses degraz.

V

Death, who have led us to that pass
Where all the lakes are frozen glass
To make us mortals slip and slide,
It's true I hate you, but alas,
I do not send you to harass:
Rather, to comfort and to guide,
To rid them of the vain, false pride
Which tireless after them will stride
And bring them to the great impasse.
Then he—who finds himself rope-tied
And feels your arms about him glide—
Impenitent, is but an ass.

VI

Morz, trai ton cor, et si le sonne
A Proneroi et a Peronne:
Fai que Bernarz primerainz l'oie,
Qui plus est près de sa coronne,
Se Dieus nel refuse et seonne
Aussi comme fausse monoie.
Morz, di li que bien sés la voie
Al jouvencel qui se desroie
Quant Damedieus santé li donne,
Et quant li tout, si le reproie:
Hors est del ploi de la coroie
Qui ne crient Dieu fors quant il tonne.

VI

Death, let your trumpeting be done
At Pronleroy and at Peronne:
First Bernard let the horn astound
Who nearest to his crown has run,
Unless God turn away to shun
A false coin, shining but unsound.
Death, tell him that your footsteps hound
The young man, wavering out of bound,
Who, though in sacred health begun,
Starts praying when it can't be found.
He's all unbuckled and unbound
Who fears but when His thunders stun.

VII

Morz, Morz, salue moi Bernart,
Mon compaignon, que Dieus me gart,
Por cui mes cuers sospire et pleure:
Di li que trop le voi coart
D'eslire a soi la meilleur part,
De torner ce desoz deseure.
Por quoi ne vient? por quoi demeure?
S'il veut que Dieus tost le sequeure,
Por quoi le veut deservir tart?
Fous atent tant que l'iaue esqueure:
Mais se il lest passer droite eure,
Dieus li dira: «Ne part ne hart!»

VII

Death, Death, salute for me Bernard,
My comrade, whom God keep and guard,
For whom my sighs and tears recur:
Tell him he must all fear discard
And choose what seems to him so hard,
To change completely or to err.
Why comes he not? Why long demur?
Should he God's quickest help prefer,
Why late to merit such regard?
Fools wait until the droughts occur,
And if he lets the hours whir
Right by him, God will say, *Trop tard*!

VIII

Morz, Morz, salue moi Renaut
De par celui qui regne en haut,
Qui se fait cremir et amer:
Di li, di li qu'il s'aparaut
A encontrer l'arc qui ne faut,
Sanz soi blecier et entamer:
C'est le jor de la mort amer,
O il covient passer la mer
Dont les ondes sont de feu chaut.
Fol puis le charpentier clamer
Qui sa maison lest a fremer
De ci la que la morz l'assaut.

VIII

O Death, salute for me Renaut,
Who through the Reign of Him may grow
To fear and love in truth for aye:
Warn him, O warn him, be not slow
To ready for that fated bow;
Unpricked, unwounded come away.
It is death's solemn, bitter day
When one must pass the sea where play
The waves in burning fire aglow.
Fool carpenter, who seeks to lay
Support beams when the old home's sway
And shiver make it death's chateau.

IX

Morz, di l'oncle, di le neveu
Qu'il nos covient par estroit treu
Passer a mout petit d'avoir.
Por ce ont sage assez en peu;
Mais li avers n'avra ja preu,
Car il ne set noient avoir.
Morz, tu nos fais apercevoir
Qu'en avoir n'a point de savoir:
Toz jorz i a del poil del leu;
Mais cil te set bien decevoir
Qui povreté set recevoir
Et queurt toz nuz a ton hareu.

IX

Uncle and nephew, Death, halloo!
Say that the needle's eye lets through
Little of all we can acquire.
The baggage of the wise is few;
No profit, misers may accrue
And nothing, nothing own entire.
O Death, you make us all admire
How gain and wisdom ill conspire:
The Devil's in their retinue.
He cheats you well who shuns desire
And will in poverty expire
To run all naked at your cue.

X

Morz, qui saisis les terres franches,
Qui fais ta queuz des gorges blanches
A ton raseor afiler,
Qui la soi a l'aver estanches,
Qui l'arbre plain de fruit esbranches
Que li riches n'ait que filer;
Qui te poines de lui guiler,
Qui par lonc mal le sés piler,
Qui li ostes al pont les planches:
Di moi a çaus d'Angiviler
Que tu fais t'aguille enfiler
Dont tu lor veus cosdre lor manches.

X

Death, who the free lands soon unfrank,
Who make of whitest throats a swank
Whetstone to trim your razor gay,
Who slake the miser's thirst in prank
And prune the ripened tree with yank
So rich man's riches fade away;
Who love to lead him long astray,
Who like to tantalize the prey,
Who tear his bridge up, plank by plank:
This message for Angiviler—
You thread your needle for that day
You'll sew their sleeves up, soiled and rank.

XI

Morz, en cui mireor se mire
L'ame, quant del cors se deschire
Et bien voit en ton livre escrit
Qu'il nos covient por Dieu eslire
Cele vie qui est la pire
Selonc le corporel delit,
Di mes amis que tuit eslit
Ont fait en paradis lor lit
Por sofrir doleur et martire.
Or facent dont ce qu'il m'ont dit!
Car ame qui Dieu ment s'ocit,
Et mout a entre faire et dire.

XI

Death, in whose mirror soul may peer
When separate from fleshly gear,
And in your book see plainly writ
How for God's sake we should revere
That life which may the worst appear
Sans worldly pleasures exquisite,
Tell all my friends the chosen flit
To paradise where beds outfit
Them after martyrdoms severe.
Now let them show they can commit,
For soul which lies to God is quit.
To talk is not to act—that's clear.

XII

Morz, qui defenz a estoier
L'avoir, que l'en doit emploier
Ançois qu'en oie tes assauz,
As princes te vueil envoier
Qui trop suelent çaus cuivroier
Qui suefrent les froiz et les chauz.
Morz, tu venges les bas des hauz
Qui tuit se sont pris a la sauz
Por saint Martin mieuz guerroier:
Tu trenches par mi a ta fauz
Faucons et ostoirs et girfauz
Que tu vois al ciel coloier.

XII

O Death, who cannot well excuse
Our hoarding assets we should use
Before we sense your knavery,
To princes I would send your news,
Those long inured to vex and bruise
Our parched and shivering misery.
Death, you avenge what plain folk see:
Great ninnies, perched up in a tree,
Who dared Saint Martin's help refuse.
You lift your cutting scythe in glee:
Those princely vultures try to flee,
Their necks stretched upward, but they lose.

XIII

Morz, qui venis de mors de pomme
Primes en femme et puis en homme,
Qui baz le siecle comme toile,
Va moi saluer la grant Romme,
Qui de rongier a droit se nomme,
Car les os ronge et le cuir poile,
Et fait a simonïaus voile
De chardonal et d'apostoile:
Romme est li mauz qui tot assomme,
Romme nos fait de siu chandoile:
Car son legat vent por estoile,
Ja tant n'ert tainz de noire gomme.

XIII

Death, who from apple bite have come
That Eve and Adam might succumb,
You hammer on a curtain frail.
Now hail the Seat of Christendom!
(Rome gnaws and nibbles, tooth and gum,
That's how she got her name)—All hail!
She weaves for simony a veil
So cardinal and pope walk hale.
Rome is the mallet strikes us numb,
Rome's tallow candles blaze and fail;
Her legate, like a star grown pale,
A dying taper has become.

XIV

Morz, fai enseler tes chevaus
Por sus metre les chardonaus,
Qui luisent comme mort charbon
Por la clarté qu'il ont en aus:
Di lor que mout ies dure a çaus
Qui plus aerdent que chardon
A bel present et a grant don
Et por ce ont chardonal non.
Romme emploie maint denier faus
Et tot fraitin et tot seon,
Et si sorargente le plon
Qu'en ne conoist les bons des maus.

XIV

Saddle your horses, Death, and ride!
Let cardinals canter at your side,
Those dying firecoals, once aflame,
Those luminaries meant to guide.
Tell them the strictest law's applied:
They want no crown of thorns but fame?
They long for luxuries and game?
Then stick them with the thistle's name!
Rome sends false money far and wide,
Worn slugs and clinkers, free of shame,
And silver coinage—who can claim
He spots the leaden heart inside?

XV

Morz, crie a Romme, crie a Rains:
«Seigneur, tuit estes en mes mains,
«Aussi li haut comme li bas.
«Ovrez voz ieuz, ceigniez voz rains,
«Ainçois que je vos praigne as frains
«Et vos face crier Hé las!
«Certes je queur plus que le pas,
«Si aport dez de deux et d'as
«Por vos faire jeter del mains.
«Laissiez voz chiflois et voz gas !
«Teus me cueve desoz ses dras
«Qui cuide estre haitiez et sains.»

XV

O Death, call out to Rome and Rheims:
'Lordlings, I handle all your schemes,
And mine are both the great and small,
Gird up your loins, wake from dreams,
Lest when I grab the bridle, screams
"Alas! Ho, help me!" rise and bawl.
The swift of foot I can forestall,
Deuces and aces I let fall
Until the man at dice blasphemes,
Leave mockery and laughter, all!
Under the cloak I snugly crawl
Of him who sound and joyful seems'.

XVI

Morz, va m'a Biauvais tot corant,
A l'evesque cui je aim tant
Et qui toz jorz m'a tenu chier:
Di li qu'il a sanz contremant
Un jor a toi, mais ne set quant;
Or se penst dont d'espeluchier
Sa vie, et sa nef espuchier
Et de bones mors aluchier.
Des ore mais se voie en grant,
Puis qu'il t'ot a son huis huchier
Por sa chaiere tresbuchier
Et por esqueurre son devant.

XVI

Now, Death, to Beauvais running pant,
To bishop whom I love descant,
The one who's always held me dear:
Say that you will quite adamant
A sudden day of life enchant,
That he should sift his hours clear
And bail his sinking bark in fear
And to good habits safely steer.
Henceforth he must be vigilant,
For at his portals you are near,
Ready to rock his throne and sneer
And filch his monies, jubilant.

XVII

Morz, qui les hauz en prison tiens
Aussi comme nos, povres chiens,
Cui li siecles a en despit:
Salue deus evesques miens
Qui sont de Noion et d'Orliens:
Di lor qu'il ont mains de respit
Qu'il n'a en lor faces escrit.
Tu fais de grant terme petit,
Or se gardent de tes engiens!
Tu prenz le dormant en son lit,
Tu tous al riche son delit,
Tu fais biauté devenir fiens.

XVII

Death, in whose fetters greatest men
Are made to us poor dogs akin
Whom generations long indict:
Salute for me my bishops twin:
At Orleans and Noyon din
My tale of how their sunlit height
Is shadowed by a coming night.
You'll tear up their reprieves in spite:
Let not your cunning take them in!
The sleeper in his bed you fright,
Cut off the rich man from delight,
Turn beauty into dung, and grin.

XVIII

Morz, qui as contes et as rois
Acorces lor anz et lor mois,
Qu'onques nus aloignier ne pout:
Chartres et Chaalons et Blois
Salue por les Tibaudois,
Loeïs, Renaut et Rotrout!
Morz, qui rehapes quanqu'en tout
Et qui menjues quanqu'en mout:
Di a mes amis, a cez trois,
Que ne prestres ne Dieus n'asout
Celui qui sa dete ne sout
Ainz que tu l'aies pris a chois.

XVIII

Death, who of every count and king
The years and months go shortening—
That time which no one can renew—
To Chartres, Chalons, Blois, now bring
Salute for Thibaudois, and wing
To Louis, Renaut and Rotrou!
Death, who recover what we drew
And gobble what we grind or grew,
Tell my three comrades this one thing,
That neither priest nor God can do
Aught for the debtor overdue
When you are crouching for your spring.

XIX

Morz qui prenz çaus sodainement
Qui cuident vivre longement
Et qui pechent en esperance:
Va moi semondre vivement
Toz noz prelaz comunement,
Lombarz, Englois et çaus de France.
Por quoi ne font sanz demorance
Justise de laie poissance
Qui Dieu guerroie apertement?
Bastons ont por faire venjance,
Et cornes en senefiance
Qu'ils doivent hurter durement.

XIX

Death, who with sudden ravishment
Take those of life so confident
They linger in their sinful trance:
Go now with sermon exigent
For all our prelates pertinent,
Lombards and English, those of France.
Why is it they do not advance
With justice for the laic lance
That wars on God, belligerent?
They've clubs to beat the recreants
And horns to signify their stance:
Hard blows may be the punishment.

XX

Morz, morz, qui ja ne seras lasse
De muer haute chose en basse:
Trop volentiers fesisse aprendre
Ambesdeus les rois, se j'osasse,
Com tu trais raseor de chasse
Por rere çaus qui ont que prendre.
Morz qui les montez fais descendre
Et qui des cors as rois fais cendre:
Tu as tramail et roiz et nasse
Por devant le haut homme tendre
Qui por sa poesté estendre
Son ombre tressaut et trespasse.

XX

Death, O Death, who never tire
Of making low things out of higher:
To both kings gladly I would wend
And daily, could I nerve acquire,
Remind them how your razor dire
The richly bearded will offend.
Death, who to monarch say, 'Descend!'
Who kingly hearts to ashes blend,
The nets are yours, the snares, the wire
Before that strong man to suspend
Who would, his power to extend,
Over his shadow leap and gyre.

XXI

Morz, tu abaz a un seul tor
Aussi le roi dedenz sa tor
Com le povre dedenz son toit:
Tu erres adès sanz sejor
Por chascun semondre a son jor
De paier Dieu trestot son droit.
Morz, tu tiens tant l'ame en destroit
Qu'ele ait paié quanqu'ele doit,
Sanz nul restor et sanz retor.
Por c'est fous qui sor s'ame acroit,
Qu'ele n'a gage qu'ele ploit,
Puis qu'ele vient nue a l'estor.

XXI

O Death, your single blow makes cower
The king within his vaulted tower,
The poor man, with a roof of thatch,
And roaming all the earth to scour,
You summon each one to that hour
He must a kingly debt dispatch.
Death, to our mortal bonds you match
The soul until she can detach
And leave what all the debts devour.
Soul mortgages, a fool might hatch,
But she has nothing to attach,
All naked in the joust for power.

XXII

Mors, mout as bien assis le monde
De totes parz a la reonde:
Tu lieves sor toz ta baniere,
Tu ne trueves qui te responde
Ne par force ne par faconde,
Tant par as espoentant chiere.
Tu nos assauz en tel maniere:
De près jetes a la perriere,
De loing menaces a la fonde.
Tu tornes ce devant derriere,
Car primeraine fais la biere
Qu'en atendoit tierce o seconde.

XXII

Death, you have laid a siege profound
To earth and compassed it around.
You lift your banner everywhere:
No human ever stands his ground,
No strength nor sweetest words that sound,
Such is your terrifying stare
And such the manner of your snare.
At hand, your catapults impair,
Afar from sling the stones rebound.
You shove the first aside and glare,
Promote the third or second heir,
And caper, heaping up his mound.

XXIII

Morz, douce as bons, as maus amere,
A l'un est large., a l'autre avere,
Les uns chace, les autres fuit.
Sovent al juevne avant fait here
Et prent le fil devant le pere
Et queut la flor devant le fruit
Et le cors bote ainz qu'il s'apuit
Et tout l'ame ainz qu'ele s'acuit
Et fiert ançois qu'ele s'apere.
Morz va comme lerres par nuit
Et l'endormi en son deduit
Semont tost, avant de lui rere.

XXIII

Death, sweet to good—to evil, drear,
Generous in that case, miser here,
Now hiding, now in hot pursuit,
Sometimes the youthful see it leer,
The son precedes the father's bier,
Flower is gathered ere the fruit;
The body, an unbroken shoot,
The soul that scarcely sinks her root,
All stricken with a logic queer.
Death is a prowler, seeking loot,
The sleeper gets a brief salute
Before death pins him down to shear.

XXIV

Morz, qui est a veüe escrite
En la vieille face despite,
Se repont bien es jovenciaus,
Et plus entor çaus se delite
Qui par fierté li dient: «Fui te!»
C'est en cez cointes damoisiaus
Qui vont as chiens et as oisiaus,
Et font homage as bons morsiaus,
Qui plus ardent que leschefrite:
A çaus gieue morz de coutiaus
Et lor afuble teus mantiaus
Qu'en plain miedi lor anuite.

XXIV

Death, who in characters concrete
On old grieved faces spells defeat,
In young folk often seeks repose,
So pleased to favor those who greet
Him proudly, 'Now, begone, you cheat!'
To hunt the careless dandy goes,
With hounds and falcons seeks the close,
Pays homage to the parts he chose,
Himself as sizzling as the meat,
But Death can carve up fancy beaus,
And wrap them in their capes to doze
Till noonday is a darkened street.

XXV

Morz, o tuit sommes en atente
Que tu nos somoignes ta rente,
Bien nos as fort loié le point:
Tu prenz celui en sa jovente,
A vint et huit anz o a trente,
Qui cuide estre en son meilleur point.
Com plus s'acesme et plus se joint,
Tost l'as de ton aguillon point
Qui plus entosche que tarente.
Por c'est droiz que chascuns ressoint,
Car cui deliz del siecle voint
Mout part de lui s'ame dolente.

XXV

Death, we expect imperilment,
That day when you will claim your rent;
You've got our hands tied from the womb.
You take the new young resident
With thirty years of age unspent,
When all the waiting hours bloom.
Despite his trappings and perfume,
You soon have pricked him to a doom
Tarantula could not invent.
Some caution must our lives illume,
For he who dances to the tomb
Can make the parting soul lament.

XXVI

Morz, en sainte ame et en eslite,
Quel char qu'ele ait, maigre o porfite,
N'a de poesté fors mout poi:
Lues qu'ele est hors, la claimme quite.
Por c'est sages qui or s'aquite,
Endementiers qu'il a de quoi;
Car en ame qui est sanz foi,
Qui lest son cors vivre sanz loi,
Morz parmenablement habite.
Or ait chascuns merci de soi,
Car qui ne prent hastif conroi
Ne puet faillir a mort sobite.

XXVI

Death over holy soul and sweet,
Lean or fat of the body's meat,
With little power wields his rod:
Her parting brings a full receipt.
Therefore it's wise to clear the sheet
Before death puts us in the sod,
For soul that has no faith in God
And lets the body lawless plod,
Death makes his favorite retreat.
Now let self-mercy each man prod,
Since he who goes so lazy-shod
May have a sudden Death to meet.

XXVII

Morz sobite est a droit nomee
Quant la vie n'est ordenee
Ançois que l'ame isse del cors;
Et ame qui si est alee,
Mieuz li venist qu'ainc ne fust nee,
Tant par trueve chier tens dehors.
Por ce n'est nus graindres tresors
Que paors Dieu par bon amors
En juevne cuer enracinee.
Queus que li cors soit, blans o sors,
Mieuz retient toz jorz celui mors
Dont l'ame est primes abevree.

XXVII

Sudden is Death, we rightly say,
When life unordered goes its way
Till soul from body seeks divorce;
And for the soul that parts astray,
Best it were never born to clay
That has from suffering no recourse.
Our greatest treasure has its source
In godly fear and love, a force
Deep rooted in young hearts to stay.
Though dark or fair, or fine or coarse,
We all remember every course
That fed the soul self yesterday.

XXVIII

Que vaut quanque li siecles fait?
Morz en une eure tot desfait,
Qui ne gieue pas a refaire.
Que vaut quanqu'avarice atrait?
Morz en une eure tot fortrait,
Qui nul gieu ne pert par mestraire.
Morz fait les plus emparlez taire,
Les enrisez plorer et braire;
Morz fait toz jorz de bel tens lait;
Morz fait valoir et sac et haire
Autant com porpre et robe vaire;
Morz contre toz desrainne a plait.

XXVIII

What good is all the worldlings make?
Death will upon the hour break
Past all remaking, all our share.
What good is all that greed can rake?
Death in an hour wins the stake—
The faultless player, fortuned fair,
Death robs the talker of his air,
The jester, sets to weep and swear,
Fine weather into foul can wake.
Sackcloth and ashes Death will pair
With purple and with ermine wear;
Death will the stand against us take.

XXIX

Que vaut biautez, que vaut richece,
Que vaut honeurs? que vaut hautece,
Puis que morz tot a sa devise
Fait sor nos pluie et secherece,
Puis qu'ele a tot en sa destrece,
Quanqu'en despist et quanqu'en prise?
Qui paor de mort a jus mise,
C'est cil cui la morz plus atise
Et vers cui ele ançois s'adrece.
Cors bien norriz, chars bien alise
Fait de vers et de feu chemise:
Qui plus s'aaise plus se blece.

XXIX

What good is Beauty, or is Ease,
Honor, what is it, if you please,
Since death can bring in his own time
Tempest or sunshine, rain or breeze,
Since he with universal squeeze
Grips the unworthy and sublime?
He who, not fearing Death, will climb,
It's he who rouses Death to crime;
He is the first one death will tease.
Fat paunches and the skin's soft prime
He coats with fire and worms and slime:
The most contented, most he sees.

XXX

Morz prueve, et je de riens n'en dot,
Qu'autant ne vaille peu com mot
De tote rien qui muert et seche.
Morz mostre que noient est tot,
Et quanque glotonie englot
Et quanque lecherie leche.
Morz fait que li sainz hom ne peche,
Por ce que riens ne li conteche
O ele puist doner un bot.
Mors met a un pris grange et creche,
Vin et iaue, saumon et seche;
Morz dit a totes aises «tprot».

XXX

Death proves until I doubt it not
Little must weigh in like a lot
Where all things wither, die and bleach.
Death shows illusion long begot,
All that old gluttony has got
And all that lechery can leech.
Death keeps the holy man from breach,
But Death's not satisfied with each
New victim of his fatal shot.
Wine, water, salmon, scum of beach,
Silo and manger—equal speech.
Death says to all our pleasures, 'Rot!'

XXXI

Morz est la roiz qui tot atrape,
Morz est la mains qui tot agrape;
Tot li remaint quanqu'ele aert.
Morz fait a toz d'isembrun chape
Et de la pure terre nape,
Morz a toz oniement sert,
Morz toz secrez met en apert,
Morz fait franc homme de cuivert,
Morz acuivertist roi et pape,
Morz rent chascun ce qu'il desert,
Morz rent al povre ce qu'il pert,
Morz tout al riche quanqu'il hape.

XXXI

Death is the net that will entrap,
Death is the hand that will us rap;
None that it touches can depart.
Death has for us a sombre wrap
And muddy blanket for our nap;
Impartially his favors dart.
Death bares all secrets of the heart,
Death hands the serf a freeman's chart,
In irons king and pope will clap.
Death renders every claim with art,
Death gives the poor man a new start,
Death leaves the rich man not a scrap.

XXXII

Morz fait a chascun sa droiture,
Morz fait a toz droite mesure,
Morz poise tot a juste pois,
Morz venge chascun de s'injure,
Morz met orgueil a porreture,
Morz fait faillir la guerre as rois,
Morz fait garder decrez et lois,
Morz fait laissier usure et crois,
Morz fait de soëf vie dure,
Morz as porees et as pois
Donne saveur de bon craspois
Es cloistres o l'en crient luxure.

XXXII

Death can our equal rights insure,
Death takes all measures just and pure,
Death's scales in honesty excel,
Death can avenge each wrong obscure,
Death gives the proud up to manure,
Death may a king in war repel.
Death seals decrees and laws full well,
Death, usury and gain may quell;
Death hardens up the epicure,
Death in the beets and peas may dwell
By just a bit of seasoning fell
In cloisters fearing lust and lure.

XXXIII

Morz apaise les ennoisiez,
Morz acoise les envoisiez,
Morz totes les meslees fine,
Morz met en croiz toz faus croisiez,
Morz fait droit a toz les boisiez,
Morz toz les plaiz a droit termine,
Morz desoivre rose d'espine,
Paille de grain, bren de farine,
Les purs vins des faus armoisiez;
Morz voit par mi voile et cortine,
Morz seule set et adevine
Com chascuns est a droit proisiez.

XXXIII

Death soothes the wranglers of each sex,
Death stills the janglers with a hex,
Death puts an end to battle spleen,
Death soon the false crusaders checks,
Death straightens out deluded wrecks,
Death judges every trial serene.
The rose and thorn, Death comes between,
The wheat from chaff he whistles clean,
The wine that's watered he rejects;
Death sees through every veil and screen,
And only Death appraises keen
The certain value of our necks.

XXXIV

Morz, honiz est qui ne te crient,
Et plus honiz cui d'el ne tient
Fors ce que vie ne li faille:
Faillir sanz faille la covient,
Peu la tendra qui plus la tient,
Quanqu'en aloigne morz retaille.
Mais li fol dient: «Nos que chaille
«De quel eure morz nos assaille?
«Prendons or le bien qui nos vient!
«Après, que puet valoir si vaille:
«Morz est la fins de la bataille
«Et ame et cors noient devient.»

XXXIV

Death, shamed be he who's insolent
And more ashamed, the man intent
On when and whether he must die,
For in this game he's impotent;
He clings to something transient.
Death shortens every long goodbye.
But fools say, 'How should we apply
Our thoughts to when Death comes and why?
Let's just enjoy the merriment,
And after, who can prophesy?
Death puts an end to battle cry,
And everything's to nothing sent.'

XXXV

Pieç'a que ceste erreurs comence:
De ceste seculer science
Dont fu la viez filosofie
Nasqui ceste pesme sentence
Qui tout a Dieu sa providence
Et dit qu'autres siecles n'est mie.
Selonc ce a meilleur partie
Cil qui s'abandonne a folie
Que cil qui garde continence.
Mais certes, s'il n'est autre vie,
Entre ame a homme et ame a truie
N'a donques point de diference.

XXXV

Of old this error did commence;
From secular intelligence
That ancient formed philosophy
Was born that wicked old pretense
Which takes from God his providence
And can no other world foresee.
If true, then it were best to be
Abandoned to debauchery
Than holding on to continence.
But sure, if heaven's absentee,
Then soul of man and pig agree
Without a bit of difference.

XXXVI

S'autres siecles n'est, donques viaus
Ait ci li cors toz ses aviaus
Et face quanque li delite:
Vive li hom comme porciaus,
Car toz pechiez est bons et biaus!
S'en vertu n'a point de merite.
Hé! que feront dont cil ermite
Qui por Dieu ont lor char aflite
Et beü tant amers jusiaus?
S'après la mort est quite quite,
Dont ont la pïeur vie eslite
Tuit cil de l'ordene de Cistiaus.

XXXVI

Were there no other life divine,
Here might the body drink and dine
And wander as its whims direct:
And man could live like any swine,
For every sin were good and fine!
Were virtue useless and suspect,
Ah, what of the poor hermit sect,
Ascetics, who in God's respect,
Have downed a bitter juice for wine?
If after death it's quits direct,
Then they are to the worst elect,
The Cîteaux brotherhood, benign.

XXXVII

Se Dieus ailleurs nul bien ne rent,
Mout chier as blans moignes se vent;
Mout ont le mieuz cil as cras cous
Qui ne tiennent Dieu nul covent,
Ainz font procession sovent
As bons morsiaus et as liz mous.
Car certes, si com dit sainz Pous,
Cil qui set dire les bons cous :
«Qui bien que puet avoir ne prent,
«Ainz suefre por Dieu les durs cous,
«Mout est maleüreus et fous
«S'il autre bien de Dieu n'atent.»

XXXVII

If God won't bless the obedient,
His cost the White Monks may lament,
While Fat Craws have a share profuse,
Who keep no godly pledge, content,
But punctual and diligent
Put sweets and downy beds to use.
For sure, as Saint Paul can adduce,
Whose words are wisdom's very juice:
'Who seizes not the good that's sent
And suffers, making God excuse,
Is but a wretched fool, obtuse,
Unless a higher good is meant.'

XXXVIII

Se Dieus ne vent repos por laste
A celui qui n'a pain ne paste
Et qui por lui s'est esilliez
En l'ordene qui le cors degaste,
Por faire l'ame sobre et chaste:
Fous est li genz, li atilliez
Qui por Dieu s'est tant avilliez
Qu'en blanc ordene s'est chevilliez,
Et qui d'aler a Dieu se haste.
Bien est dont sainz Lorenz truilliez
Qui fu rostiz et graeilliez
Et fist por Dieu de son cors haste.

XXXVIII

If God rests not the pain-embraced
Who long for bread and meat to taste
And who for Him go poorly fed
In order which will body waste
To make a spirit sober, chaste,
Then foolish is that youth, fine-bred,
Who lowers unto God his head
And quickly in White Order's sped
And humbly after God makes haste.
Saint Lawrence must have been misled,
Roasted and grilled till he was dead
And turned upon the spit to baste.

XXXIX

Bien nos ont mostré tuit li saint,
Qui tant furent por Dieu destraint,
Que ce que Dieus dist n'est pas fable,
Ne que n'est contrové ne faint
Ce que sainte Escriture a paint
De mort, de vie parmenable.
Bien ont doné tesmoing creable
Que li torment sont pardurable
O cil iront cui la chars vaint.
Or sont assis a la grant table,
Prince del ciel et conestable:
Qui honeur chace, honeur ataint.

XXXIX

Well have they shown us, every saint,
Who were for God so long distraint,
God's word cannot a fable be,
Invented nor imagined quaint—
Those pictures that the gospels paint
Of death and immortality.
Their testimony makes us see
The torments of eternity
For those who bear the body's taint.
Round heaven's table sit the free,
Great princes of integrity:
They beckon, but there's no constraint.

XL

Morz, se riche homme a toi pensassent,
Ja lor ames la n'engajassent
O n'a mestier ors ne argenz:
Ja lor vius cors si n'aaisassent
Ne lor ongles si n'aguisassent
Por escorchier les povres genz,
Car en çaus fiches tu tes denz
Plus en parfont et plus dedenz
Qui a tort travaillent et lassent
Les abandonez a toz venz,
Qui de la sustance as dolenz
La fain d'avarice respassent.

XL

Death, if on you the rich had cast
A thought, they'd not have pawned so fast
Their souls where gold or silver's weak;
Nor pampered bodies to the last,
Nor filed their talons for repast
To skin the paupers and the meek.
With sharpest teeth in them you speak
And gnaw them in a style unique,
Those folk who burden, all aghast,
Poor wretches whom the raw winds seek;
Those misers who on pinched and bleak
Have fed a hunger unsurpassed.

XLI

Morz, tu defies et guerroies
Çaus qui des tailles et des proies
Font les sorfaiz et les outrages:
Toz tes tormenz en çaus emploies
Qui d'autrui doleur font lor joies.
Neporquant c'est mais li usages
(Ce pert par tot as seignorages),
Icist tempez, icist orages
Chace lor ames males voies.
Hé! certes, c'est uns vasselages
Faire son preu d'autrui damages
Et d'autrui cuir larges coroies!

XLI

Death, your defiant arms deploy
Toward those who tax and pilfer coy
And plunder in their brigandage;
You with your torments folk annoy
Who from man's sorrow take their joy,
And yet these customs grow with age,
Touch those of highborn lineage,
As if some tempest's howling rage
Had plucked the souls up to destroy.
Ah, what a noble personage
Is he who profits from outrage
And callous, will man's hide employ!

XLII

Morz, tu queurs la o orgueus fume
Por esteindre quanqu'il alume;
Tes ongles, sanz oster, enz fiches
El riche, qui art et escume
Sor le povre, cui sanc il hume.
Ha! Richece, por quoi nos triches?
Qui plus a bacons plus tout fliches,
Qui plus a gastiaus plus tout miches.
Certes, teus est mais la costume:
Quant plus est li hom fors et riches,
Tant est il plus avers et chiches,
Et plus a froit qui plus a plume.

XLII

O Death, you hasten to pride's fume
To smother, lest its flames relume;
Your nails inexorable niche
In those who ever burn and spume
And may the poor man's blood consume.
Ha! Why deceive us, calling 'Rich'?
Who owns a ham, will bacon snitch,
And who has cakes, for bread will itch.
It is the custom, we presume:
And strange to say, the more we switch
To wealth, the more the pennies witch,
And colder is he, wrapped in plume.

XLIII

Li mieuz vestu et li plus cras
Çaus a peu pain et a peu dras
Poilent adès, mais ce nos prueve
Que Dieus sanz faille, o il n'est pas,
O il les hauz juge et les bas,
Lues qu'il issent de ceste esprueve
Et rendent l'ame, viez o nueve,
Qui toz ses biens et ses maus trueve
Quant ele est venue al trespas;
Iluec aprent ele et esprueve
Que faire estuet ce que Dieus rueve:
Hom n'est pas faiz por vivre a gas.

XLIII

The better dressed and fat of face
Skin persons starving in disgrace,
Strip shabby beggars, but it proves
That either God is not nor grace
Or he must judge both high and base,
And when it seems their trial behooves,
Then Death the young and old removes
And lets the soul see all its moves,
All records of its mortal race:
From this it learns what naught disproves,
That it must do what God approves,
For life is not a jesting place.

XLIV

Dieus, qui nos forma uns et uns,
O il est et fel et enfruns
Al povre, o il est ses vengierres;
Car ce voit bien as ieuz chascuns
Que meilleur de soi dampne aucuns.
De Noiron, qui tant fu pechierres
Fu dampnez mes sire Sainz Pierres:
Cil fu sor toz fel et lechierres
Et plus ot de ses buens que nuns;
Cist sainz, et quant il fu peschierres
Et puis qu'il devint preechierres,
Fu toz jorz de toz biens jeüns.

XLIV

God, who has made us, every one,
Either has naught of benison
For poor men, or avenges care;
For each has seen a paragon
By his inferior undone.
Take Nero, thought a sinner rare,
Who damned beloved Saint Pierre;
That cruel emperor got to share
In worldly comforts by the ton,
While saint, the fisherman threadbare,
And then the holy man at prayer,
Went stripped of all the world has spun.

XLV

Mout fu li tens cez deus divers:
A l'un estez, a l'autre ivers;
Cil fu loez, cist laidengiez,
Paradis fu l'un, l'autre enfers;
Cist fu en buies et en fers,
Cil ne fu onques mis en giez;
Cil fu de toz biens aengiez,
Cestui fu toz biens chalengiez.
Dieus! cil leus devora tes sers,
Cist aigniaus fu par lui mengiez.
Certes, s'or n'est par toi vengiez,
Dont ies tu jugierres pervers.

XLV

Life was indeed for them diverse:
Summer and winter, all inverse;
This one had praise and that one, threat;
Paradise, here; there, Hell's reverse.
The one felt chains and irons coerce,
The other knew no shackle's fret.
The one had never need nor debt,
The other was by need beset.
O God! This wolf your sons will curse
And eat them like the lamb he met,
And if you don't avenge them yet,
You are a wicked judge, perverse.

XLVI

Mais, qui demande plus aperte
Venjance que la descoverte
En plain marchié, en plaine foire?
Pieç'a que sainte Eglise est certe
Queus est de chascun la deserte:
Miracle espès mostrent la gloire
O cist est venuz par victoire;
Et ce meïsme nos fait croire
Qu'or est cil cheüz en poverte,
Qui venuz est a l'amer boire
En chartre tenebreuse et noire
O nus ne recuevre sa perte.

XLVI

But who could ask for more overt
Revenge than what good men assert
In fairs and markets' common lore?
For years the Church has been expert
In judging of each man's desert.
Since puffery we have galore
To show one triumphed in this score,
The sad facts leave us to deplore
The contrast with a saint so hurt,
Constrained a bitter drink to pour,
Chained in a sunless dungeon's core
From which not one retrieves his shirt.

XLVII

Cil qui tant livres et tant mars
De l'avoir, par le monde espars,
Toloit a destre et a senestre,
Qui les vendoises et les chars,
Mulez, saumons, esturjons, bars
Faisoit desor sa table nestre,
Qui tant mist en vestir et pestre
Son cors vil et puant et flestre,
Qui n'aloit onques sanz mil chars,
Qui sogiez a Dieu ne vout estre;
Or a le feu d'enfer a mestre:
Mal est chaufez qui toz est ars.

XLVII

He who so many golden bars
And coins earth scattered from its jars
Had robbed on either hand in greed;
Who planned his gourmet repertoires
With bass and salmon as the stars
But mullet, sturgeon, carp at need;
Who wasted much to clothe and feed
His body, rotting like a weed,
Whose going took a thousand cars;
Who never wanted God to lead,
Now Master Hellfire has for meed,
And he is very warm who chars.

XLVIII

Se cil qui les gregneurs biens ont
En cest siecle et les granz maus font,
S'en alassent si sanz juise
Et passassent si quite al pont
Com cil qui par mesaise vont
A l'aise que Dieus a pramise,
Dont deïsse j'en plainne eglise
Que Dieus n'eüst point de justise.
Mais si n'iert pas, ainçois ravront
Li gros poisson la lor assise,
Qui or menjuent la menuise
Ne de nului jugié ne sont.

XLVIII

If those in worldly goods so stout
Who flaunt their evil roundabout
Unjudged, had gathered their increase
And freely passed the bridge without
Like those who suffer pain, devout,
Since God had promised them release,
Right then in church I'd never cease
To say His justice was caprice.
That will not be. Their turn will out.
Justice will claim those fish obese
Who eat the little ones in peace
And go unjudged of any doubt.

XLIX

Tuit atendons comunement
Primes mort et puis jugement:
Contre cez deus n'a qu'un confort,
C'est repentir isnelement
Et purgier soi parfaitement
De quanque li cuers se remort.
Qui ce ne fait devant la mort
A tart se plaindra et a tort
Quant Dieus en prendra vengement;
Ainz qu'en mueve la nef del port
La doit en joindre si tres fort
Qu'en voist par mer seürement.

XLIX

For all a common fate must loom,
First death and then the day of doom:
Against them we have one resort—
We must repent before the tomb
And purity again resume
And purge what conscience may report.
Who waits until his life's cut short
Will wrongly with his grief consort
When summoned to the judgment room.
Before the vessel sails from port,
If you have caulked her, she will thwart
The waves from bringing her to gloom.

L

Hé, Dieus! por qu'est tant desiree
Joie charneus envenimee,
Qui si corront nostre nature
Et qui a si corte duree?
Après est si chier comparee!
Comme est mal cele pointure
Qui fait l'ame acroire a usure
Amertume qui toz jorz dure
Por douceur qui lues est alee!
Fui, lecherie! Fui, luxure!
De si chier morsel n'ai je cure,
Mieuz aim mes pois et ma poree.

L

Oh, God! why should they be desired,
The poisoned fleshly joys acquired
Which make our nature so impure
And are of ragged time attired?
After they are so dearly hired!
How fatal is their overture
Which makes the eager soul procure
A bitterness that will endure
When every bit of joy's expired.
Fie, gluttony and lust and lure!
I gladly from your feast am poor
Unto my beets and peas retired.

BIOGRAPHICAL NOTES

The work of american poet Jenny Lind Porter was first discovered and published by Dr Ralph Tyler Flewelling, editor of the international quarterly, *The Personalist*, and founder of the Hoose Library of Philosophy at The University of Southern California. Her first translation, of Ronsard's *De l'election de son sepulcre*, appeared in *The Personalist* as did her prose poem, *The Valleys of Morning*, later interpreted in dance by Ruth St. Denis and her pupils. The Flewelling-Porter literary correspondence has been preserved in the archives of the USC Library.

Jenny Lind Porter earned BA and MA degrees from Texas Christian University and the Ph.D. in English from The University of Texas at Austin. She also completed three years of studies toward a second doctorate in Romance Languages. Pepperdine University conferred upon her an honorary doctorate.

Among her many published works are the illustrated *Three Dramatic Monologues: da Vinci, Michelangelo, Rembrandt* and *The Siege of the Alamo* (both from Pepperdine University Press), *The American Poets' Corner in the Cathedral of St. John the Divine, New York*, and *Time to Write: How William Sidney Porter Became O. Henry*, co-authored with Trueman E. O'Quinn.

Among her awards are the prestigious Alice Fay di Castagnola Award of the Poetry Society of America, selection as the Poet Laureate of Texas, the Piper Professor Award as one of the ten outstanding college professors of Texas, and an Outstanding Women of Texas Award from the American Association of University Women. She was also named to the Texas Women's Hall of Fame and elected to the Texas Philosophical Society. In 1996 the Mayor and the City

Council of Austin named 11 September Jenny Lind Porter Day in Austin in honor of her contributions to the O. Henry Museum and the Austin History Center and to scholarship on the famous master of the american short story who is her distant cousin.

Jenny Lind Porter and her husband, Lawrence E. Scott, make their home in Austin, Texas.

CISTERCIAN PUBLICATIONS, INC.
TITLES LISTING

—CISTERCIAN TEXTS—

BERNARD OF CLAIRVAUX

Apologia to Abbot William
Bernard of Clairvaux, Letters of
Five Books on Consideration: Advice to a Pope
Homilies in Praise of the Blessed Virgin Mary
Life and Death of Saint Malachy the Irishman
Love without Measure: Extracts from the Writings of St Bernard (Paul Dimier)
On Grace and Free Choice
On Loving God (Analysis by Emero Stiegman)
Parables and Sentences (Michael Casey)
Sermons for the Summer Season
Sermons on Conversion
Sermons on the Song of Songs I-IV
The Steps of Humility and Pride

WILLIAM OF SAINT THIERRY

The Enigma of Faith
Exposition on the Epistle to the Romans
Exposition on the Song of Songs
The Golden Epistle
The Mirror of Faith
The Nature and Dignity of Love
On Contemplating God: Prayer & Meditations

AELRED OF RIEVAULX

Dialogue on the Soul
Liturgical Sermons, I
Mirror of Charity
Spiritual Friendship
Treatises I: On Jesus at the Age of Twelve, Rule for a Recluse, The Pastoral Prayer
Walter Daniel: The Life of Aelred of Rievaulx

JOHN OF FORD

Sermons on the Final Verses of the Songs of Songs I-VII

GILBERT OF HOYLAND

Sermons on the Songs of Songs I-III
Treatises, Sermons and Epistles

OTHER EARLY CISTERCIAN WRITERS

Adam of Perseigne, Letters of
Alan of Lille: The Art of Preaching
Amadeus of Lausanne: Homilies in Praise of Blessed Mary
Baldwin of Ford: Spiritual Tractates I-II
Gertrud the Great: Spiritual Exercises
Gertrud the Great: The Herald of God's Loving-Kindness
Guerric of Igny: Liturgical Sermons I-[II]
Helinand of Froidmont: Verses on Death
Idung of Prüfening: Cistercians and Cluniacs: The Case for Cîteaux
Isaac of Stella: Sermons on the Christian Year, I-[II]
The Life of Beatrice of Nazareth
Serlo of Wilton & Serlo of Savigny: Seven Unpublished Works
Stephen of Lexington: Letters from Ireland
Stephen of Sawley: Treatises

—MONASTIC TEXTS—

EASTERN CHRISTIAN TRADITION

Besa: The Life of Shenoute
Cyril of Scythopolis: Lives of the Monks of Palestine
Dorotheos of Gaza: Discourses and Sayings
Evagrius Ponticus: Praktikos and Chapters on Prayer
Handmaids of the Lord: Lives of Holy Women in Late Antiquity & Early Middle Ages (Joan Petersen)
Harlots of the Desert (Benedicta Ward)
John Moschos: The Spiritual Meadow
Lives of the Desert Fathers
Lives of Simeon Stylites (Robert Doran)
Luminous Eye (Sebastian Brock)
Mena of Nikiou: Isaac of Alexandra & St Macrobius
Pachomian Koinonia I-III (Armand Veilleux)
Paphnutius: Histories/Monks of Upper Egypt
Sayings of the Desert Fathers (Benedicta Ward)
Spiritual Direction in the Early Christian East (Irénée Hausherr)
Spiritually Beneficial Tales of Paul, Bishop of Monembasia (John Wortley)
Symeon the New Theologian: The Theological and Practical Treatises & The Three Theological Discourses (Paul McGuckin)
Theodoret of Cyrrhus: A History of the Monks of Syria
The Syriac Fathers on Prayer and the Spiritual Life (Sebastian Brock)

WESTERN CHRISTIAN TRADITION

Anselm of Canterbury: Letters I-III (Walter Fröhlich)
Bede: Commentary...Acts of the Apostles
Bede: Commentary...Seven Catholic Epistles
Bede: Homilies on the Gospels III
The Celtic Monk (U. Ó Maidín)
Gregory the Great: Forty Gospel Homilies
Life of the Jura Fathers
Maxims of Stephen of Muret

CISTERCIAN PUBLICATIONS, INC.
TITLES LISTING

Meditations of Guigo I, Prior of the Charterhouse (A. Gordon Mursall)
Peter of Celle: Selected Works
Letters of Rancé I–II
Rule of the Master
Rule of Saint Augustine
Wound of Love: A Carthusian Miscellany

CHRISTIAN SPIRITUALITY

Cloud of Witnesses: The Development of Christian Doctrine (David N. Bell)
Call of Wild Geese (Matthew Kelty)
Cistercian Way (André Louf)
The Contemplative Path
Drinking From the Hidden Fountain (Thomas Špidlík)
Eros and Allegory: Medieval Exegesis of the Song of Songs (Denys Turner)
Fathers Talking (Aelred Squire)
Friendship and Community (Brian McGuire)
From Cloister to Classroom
Life of St Mary Magdalene and of Her Sister St Martha (David Mycoff)
Many Mansions (David N. Bell)
Mercy in Weakness (André Louf)
Name of Jesus (Irénée Hausherr)
No Moment Too Small (Norvene Vest)
Penthos: The Doctrine of Compunction in the Christian East (Irénée Hausherr)
Rancé and the Trappist Legacy (A.J. Krailsheimer)
Russian Mystics (Sergius Bolshakoff)
Sermons in a Monastery (Matthew Kelty)
Silent Herald of Unity: The Life of Maria Gabrielle Sagheddu (Martha Driscoll)
Spirituality of the Christian East (Thomas Špidlík)
Spirituality of the Medieval West (André Vauchez)
Tuning In To Grace (André Louf)
Wholly Animals: A Book of Beastly Tales (David N. Bell)

—MONASTIC STUDIES—

Community and Abbot in the Rule of St Benedict I–II (Adalbert de Vogüé)
Finances of the Cistercian Order in the Fourteenth Century (Peter King)
Fountains Abbey and Its Benefactors (Joan Wardrop)
The Hermit Monks of Grandmont (Carole A. Hutchison)
In the Unity of the Holy Spirit (Sighard Kleiner)
Joy of Learning & the Love of God: Essays in Honor of Jean Leclercq
Monastic Odyssey (Marie Kervingant)
Monastic Practices (Charles Cummings)
Occupation of Celtic Sites in Ireland (Geraldine Carville)
Reading St Benedict (Adalbert de Vogüé)
Rule of St Benedict: A Doctrinal and Spiritual Commentary (Adalbert de Vogüé)
Rule of St Benedict (Br. Pinocchio)
St Hugh of Lincoln (David H. Farmer)
Stones Laid Before the Lord (Anselme Dimier)
Venerable Bede (Benedicta Ward)
What Nuns Read (David N. Bell)
With Greater Liberty: A Short History of Christian Monasticism & Religious Orders (Karl Frank)

—CISTERCIAN STUDIES—

Aelred of Rievaulx: A Study (Aelred Squire)
Athirst for God: Spiritual Desire in Bernard of Clairvaux's Sermons on the Song of Songs (Michael Casey)
Beatrice of Nazareth in Her Context (Roger De Ganck)
Bernard of Clairvaux: Man, Monk, Mystic (Michael Casey) [tapes and readings]
Bernardus Magister (Nonacentenary)
Catalogue of Manuscripts in the Obrecht Collection of the Institute of Cistercian Studies (Anna Kirkwood)
Christ the Way: The Christology of Guerric of Igny (John Morson)
Cistercian Abbeys of Britain
Cistercians in Denmark (Brian McGuire)
Cistercians in Medieval Art (James France)
Cistercians in Scandinavia (James France)
A Difficult Saint (Brian McGuire)
Dore Abbey (Shoesmith & Richardson)
A Gathering of Friends: Learning & Spirituality in John of Forde (Costello and Holdsworth)
Image and Likeness: The Augustinian Spirituality of William of St Thierry (David Bell)
Index of Authors & Works in Cistercian Libraries in Great Britain I (David Bell)
Index of Cistercian Authors and Works in Medieval Library Catalogues in Great Britian (David Bell)
Mystical Theology of St Bernard (Étienne Gilson)
The New Monastery: Texts & Studies on the Earliest Cistercians
Nicolas Cotheret's Annals of Cîteaux (Louis J. Lekai)
Pater Bernhardus (Franz Posset)
A Second Look at Saint Bernard (Jean Leclercq)
The Spiritual Teachings of St Bernard of Clairvaux (John R. Sommerfeldt)

CISTERCIAN PUBLICATIONS, INC.
TITLES LISTING

Studies in Medieval Cistercian History (various)
Studiosorum Speculum (Louis J. Lekai)
Three Founders of Cîteaux
(Jean-Baptiste Van Damme)
Towards Unification with God (Beatrice of Nazareth in Her Context, 2)
William, Abbot of St Thierry
Women and St Bernard of Clairvaux
(Jean Leclercq)

MEDIEVAL RELIGIOUS —WOMEN—

Lillian Thomas Shank and John A. Nichols, editors

Distant Echoes
Hidden Springs: Cistercian Monastic Women
(2 volumes)
Peace Weavers

—CARTHUSIAN— TRADITION

Call of Silent Love (A Carthusian)
Freedom of Obedience (A Carthusian)
Guigo II: The Ladder of Monks & Twelve Meditations (Colledge & Walsh)
Interior Prayer (A Carthusian)
Meditations of Guigo II (A. Gordon Mursall)
Prayer of Love and Silence (A Carthusian)
Way of Silent Love (A Carthusian Miscellany)
Wound of Love (A Carthusian Miscellany)
They Speak by Silences (A Carthusian)
Where Silence is Praise (A Carthusian)

-STUDIES IN CISTERCIAN- ART & ARCHITECTURE

Meredith Parsons Lillich, editor

Volumes II-V are now available

—THOMAS MERTON—

Climate of Monastic Prayer (T. Merton)
Legacy of Thomas Merton (P. Hart)
Message of Thomas Merton (P. Hart)
Monastic Journey of Thomas Merton (P. Hart)
Thomas Merton/Monk (P. Hart)
Thomas Merton on St Bernard
Toward an Integrated Humanity
(M. Basil Pennington, ed.)

CISTERCIAN LITURGICAL —DOCUMENTS SERIES—

Chrysogonus Waddell, ocso, editor

Hymn Collection of the...Paraclete
Institutiones nostrae: The Paraclete Statutes
Molesme Summer-Season Breviary (4 volumes)
Old French Ordinary & Breviary of the Abbey of the Paraclete (2 volumes)
Twelfth-century Cistercian Hymnal
(2 volumes)
The Twelfth-century Cistercian Psalter
Two Early Cistercian *Libelli Missarum*

-STUDIA PATRISTICA XVIII-

Volumes 1, 2 and 3

Editorial queries & advance book information should be directed to the Editorial Offices:

Cistercian Publications
1201 Oliver Street
Western Michigan University
Kalamazoo, Michigan 49008
Tel: (616) 387-8920 • Fax: (616) 387-8921

• • •

Customers may order these books through booksellers or directly by contacting the warehouse at the address below:

Cistercian Publications
Saint Joseph's Abbey
167 North Spencer Road
Spencer, Massachusetts 01562-1233
Tel: (508) 885-8730 • Fax: (508) 885-4687
email: cistpub@spencerabbey.org

• • •

Canadian Orders:
Novalis
49 Front Street East, Second Floor
Toronto, Ontario M5E 1B3
Telephone: 416-363-3303 1-800-387-7164
Fax: 416-363-9409

• • •

British & European Orders:
Cistercian Publications
Mount Saint Bernard Abbey
Coalville, Leicester LE67 5UL
Fax: [44] (1530) 81.46.08

• • •

Cistercian Publications is a non-profit corporation. Its publishing program is restricted to monastic texts in translation and books on the monastic tradition.

A complete catalogue of texts in translation and studies on early, medieval, and modern monasticism is available, free of charge, by contacting any of the addresses above.